Narita Bahra QC is a leading defence ba
heavyweight and high-profile Business Cr.
as an effective tactician in the field of Business Crime and financial
services. Her stellar work ethic results in tangible impact and defining
successful outcomes in cases involving fraud, tax evasion, money
laundering and Anti-competitive conduct (cartels, market abuse, insider
dealing), investment products (carbon credits, diamonds, bitcoin) and
Confiscation.

She is noted for handling fraud cases with an international dimension,
particularly in Southeast Asia. Narita is recognised as having vast and
practical knowledge of the increasing prosecutions involving the Hawala
banking system.

Specialism in this field requires an updated and excellent knowledge of
financial proceedings such as confiscation, asset forfeiture and restraint
law.

www.naritabahra.com

David Winch B.Com., F.C.A. is a forensic accountant specialising in
crime and proceeds of crime and a sought-after commentator on
confiscation and money laundering, appearing on national television and
radio. A chartered accountant and a leading member of the team at
Sedulo Forensic Accountants, he has appeared as an expert witness in
Crown Courts, the High Court, the First Tier Tribunal (Tax Chamber),
and the Royal Court (Jersey). In the Crown Court he has given evidence
in leading confiscation cases, including *R v Harvey [2015] UKSC
73* and *Boyle Transport (Northern Ireland) Ltd v R [2016] EWCA Crim
19*. David is the author of numerous webinars and blogs on confiscation
and was joint author (with Janet Bazley of 1 Garden Court Chambers)
of '*Money Laundering for Lawyers: the new requirements and their practical
implications*' published by Butterworths (2004).

www.seduloforensic.co.uk

John Carl Townsend is recognised as a specialist in the field of POCA and asset forfeiture. He has acted in all proceedings connected to the Proceeds of Crime Act 2002 including Part 5 (Asset Forfeiture) and Part 6 (Tax). He is a tenant at 33 Chancery Lane.

His practice encompasses the civil and criminal courts with a focus on complex and high value financial investigations. In the civil courts he acts for claimant and defendant companies and individuals in claims relating to allegations of breach of fiduciary duty, unlawful means conspiracy and deceit. In the criminal courts he provides advice and representation in fraud and money laundering prosecutions. He is frequently retained in cases where there is the potential for both civil and criminal liability.

John Carl has acted for clients in respect of international freezing orders, restraint orders, civil disclosure orders (including Norwich Pharmacal and Bankers Trust), account freezing orders, unexplained wealth orders, judicial review, tax tribunals, SFO s.2 investigations, allegations of regulatory breach and goods seizures as a result of alleged duty evasion.

https://www.33knowledge.com/john-carl-townsend

A Practical Guide to Confiscation and Restraint

A Practical Guide to Confiscation and Restraint

Narita Bahra QC
33 Chancery Lane
Garrick Law

David Winch B.Com., F.C.A.
Forensic Accountant
Sedulo Forensic Accountants

John Carl Townsend
Barrister
33 Chancery Lane

Law Brief Publishing

Published 2022 by Law Brief Publishing, an imprint of Law Brief Publishing Ltd
30 The Parks
Minehead
Somerset
TA24 8BT

www.lawbriefpublishing.com

Paperback: 978-1-913715-44-1

FOREWORD

The Proceeds of Crime Act 2002 includes the confiscation regime and a wide range of powers designed to assist in removing the proceeds of crime from those who are in possession of them. It is a complex Act and a complex scheme. Practitioners are often intimidated by it and mistakes are common. The Law Commission's Consultation Paper No. 249 explains the problems in the current system.

It is a great achievement to create a short guide to this area. Judges often say that they wish they had enough time to write short judgments. It takes effort and skill, and the result is more useful because it is clear and accessible. This book will be of great value for just that reason. Practitioners will do well to carry it with them and use it as their first port of call to guide them in the right direction. It will save them from error and give them confidence to tackle cases which may at first seem intractable. If they take the time to read it all, they will get a grasp of the whole scheme and realise that it is not quite as full of traps and banana skins as it may seem.

The authors are to be congratulated for producing this work which is based on this very sound concept, and which should improve decision making at all stages of the proceedings.

Lord Justice Edis
December 2021

.

PREFACE

Having practised at the Criminal Bar for in excess of 20 years now, the landscape in relation to financial crime and ensuing financially ancillary orders has dramatically changed. Unfortunately, so has the remuneration for undertaking such tasks due to the cuts to Legal Aid funding, often resulting in financial orders being an afterthought. If financial proceedings are kept at the forefront of the practitioner's mind when undertaking the criminal proceedings and at the early stages of the case, it is highly likely that the lay client will achieve the best outcome. It became clear to me upon researching that there was no user friendly practitioner's handbook which provided a reference toolkit, which could be easily accessed at each stage of preparing the case. That was when I pitched my idea to my professional colleagues, David Winch and John Townsend, who can always be relied upon to establish the answer to all those difficult financial remedy scenarios.

As you will appreciate the scope of financial remedies and proceedings is vast. We therefore, decided to focus on the scenarios which practitioners are most likely to encounter in the courts in 2021 and beyond. The law is believed to be correct as at 1 November 2021. Except where indicated, the law and practice is that of England and Wales and statutory references are to Part 2, Proceeds of Crime Act 2002, as amended.

We have kept in mind the lawyer who may not have had too much experience in dealing with confiscation and restraint. We have aimed to be helpful without being patronising and accurate without simply reciting statute. Footnotes have been used extensively to signpost authorities and further reading. Occasionally we have employed simplified fictional worked examples to ensure the meaning is clear.

We hope that we have been successful in achieving our aim. Happy prepping.

Narita Bahra QC
David Winch
John Townsend
December 2021

CONTENTS

INTRODUCTION

Confiscation "the action of taking or seizing
someone's property with authority"

Financial Restraint "restricts the freedom or prevents
the movements of monies".

It would be so simple if confiscation proceedings resulted in simply recouping proceeds or property unlawfully gained. However, the legislation is complex and the effect can be draconian.

Looking back briefly to the last century, the Drug Trafficking Offences Act 1986 (effective 12 January 1987) introduced confiscation that was limited to drug trafficking offences alone. The Criminal Justice Act 1988 allowed courts to confiscate proceedings of non-drug indictable offences and specified summary offences. The confiscation provisions in relation to drug trafficking offences were strengthened by the Criminal Justice (International Co-operation) Act 1990 and later by the Drug Trafficking Act 1994. The confiscation provisions for non-drug offences were also strengthened, by the Proceeds of Crime Act 1995 in particular.

By the year 2000 the combination of different legislation for drug and non-drug related confiscation was recognised as being overly complex and exacerbated by the involvement of both the High Court and the Crown Court in confiscation proceedings. Confiscation was generally seen as ineffective.

The Proceeds of Crime Act 2002 (the confiscation and restraint provisions of which came into force on 24 March 2003) was intended to provide a more effective and comprehensive legislative framework. It results in the Crown Court having to mandatorily proceed with a POCA confiscation hearing if the defendant is convicted of an offence, and either the prosecutor has asked the court to proceed or the Court believes it is appropriate to do so[1].

The world of confiscation under POCA is sometimes likened to the world explored by Alice after she passed 'Through the Looking-Glass'. In criminal proceedings the burden ordinarily rests upon the prosecution to prove matters to the criminal standard. In confiscation proceedings the burden often falls on the defendant, and to the civil standard.

Worse, in this world, as Humpty Dumpty said, "When I use a word it means just what I choose it to mean — neither more nor less". So, we find that a defendant's benefit is not the amount by which he has benefited, his available amount is not the amount he has available to satisfy a confiscation order, he may have a criminal lifestyle without a lifestyle of crime, a tainted gift may be neither tainted nor a gift, and the amount ordered to be recovered from him may not be the recoverable amount. To top it all, a confiscation order does not actually confiscate anything.

POCA is not limited to assets within the UK. Overseas assets held by a UK defendant can be used to satisfy a confiscation order. Indeed, POCA permits the making of a confiscation order requiring payment of the full amount of the defendant's benefit even where no property of his has been identified which would enable him to pay that sum. This is sometimes referred to as a finding that the defendant has hidden assets.

The landscape of confiscation and restraint has evolved dramatically over the last 20 years as a result of new statute and case law. The impact of confiscation can be devastating although these orders are not deemed punitive. Prosecutors are encouraged to focus on possible confiscation proceedings at the outset of an investigation and financial recoupment is becoming a critical factor in the decision-making process as to whether to investigate and/or charge individuals with acquisitive crime or even regulatory offences. It is, therefore, essential that those who defend in criminal proceedings have confiscation and restraint at the forefront of their mind, when making key decisions in a case. A failure to do so can

---

[1] POCA s6(1), (2) & (3)

have a detrimental, and irreversible, impact on the client's finances, family life and liberty.

In this practitioner's guidebook we first seek to take a closer look at the investigation and charging process. We seek to set out what factors those prosecuting and defending should bear in mind when applying for restraint orders. We briefly outline the potential dangers of a trial and pleas impacting on the final confiscation outcome. There are significant factors which should be considered to ensure that the best outcome remains achievable, even at the early stages of an investigation or case. We consider the benefits of Legal Aid versus private representation. We have provided templates and proformas to assist those preparing responses in confiscation proceedings. We demystify the Humpty Dumpty expressions.

With the pursuit of confiscation and restraint proceedings by prosecuting authorities, expert witnesses are regularly being instructed by both parties. It is imperative that all expert witnesses instructed are aware of their expert duties, whether under statute, the Criminal Procedure Rules, or their own professional standards, and comply with them fully.

We set out the procedure of confiscation hearings and applications to vary confiscation orders. A simple guide to sentences in default is provided and guidance on steps to take when activating a sentence in default is under consideration.

We also address the slightly more unusual situations such as a defendant absconding prior to the confiscation proceedings, appeals, second confiscation proceedings and close with an introduction to account freezing and account forfeiture orders.

CHAPTER ONE

INVESTIGATION AND CHARGING

There are a multitude of matters to be taken into consideration prior to the charging of an alleged offender with one or more offences. The purpose of this chapter is to highlight some of the factors that are relevant, even at this early stage, to proceedings that are connected to the proceeds of crime.

Investigatory powers under Part 8, POCA 2002

Where the suspected offending may include a money laundering offence (that is an offence under sections 327, 328 or 329 POCA), or there is detained cash, detained property, or frozen funds investigation (within the meaning of s.341) and in specified other circumstances, the investigatory powers of Part 8, PoCA 2002 may be available.

One of the most commonly used of these is the power to obtain a production order[2] requiring a third party (such as a bank, an accountant, or a solicitor) to produce material sought for the purposes of the investigation.

A production order may, and usually should, be made following an *ex parte* application[3] and has the advantage that the material may be obtained by the investigator without alerting the suspected offender to the existence of an investigation. However where a production order is served on a bank the bank may then freeze their customer's accounts (so alerting the suspected offender to the possibility that he is under investigation) as the bank may then have a suspicion of money laundering.

---

[2] s345

[3] s351(1)

A person subject to a production order is prohibited from notifying the suspected offender of the existence of the production order where he knows or suspects this disclosure would be likely to prejudice the investigation[4]. It is good practice to bring this prohibition to the attention of any person served with a production order.

Material obtained under a production order may be used in evidence at trial.

Material subject to legal professional privilege[5], and excluded material[6], cannot be obtained by a production order, but documents such as a solicitor's conveyancing file are not normally privileged and so can be obtained.

Material held by HMRC may be obtained under other legislation[7]. The material held by HMRC is not limited to that from self-assessment income tax returns, but can include VAT return information, company tax returns and accounts (usually providing more detail than accounts filed at Companies House), and third-party information – all of which may assist in the investigation and may be used in evidence at trial.

Part 8, POCA 2002 also contains a variety of other powers, including search and seizure powers.

Restraint orders

Where the suspected offender has valuable assets and may ultimately be the subject of confiscation proceedings, it may be appropriate to obtain a restraint order[8] which will have the effect of preventing the transfer, removal, or dissipation of those assets.

---

[4] s342

[5] s348(1) & (2)

[6] s348(3), s379 & Police and Criminal Evidence Act 1984

[7] Including s19 Anti-terrorism, Crime and Security Act 2001

[8] s41

Whilst a restraint order may be obtained *ex parte*, it is necessary to promptly serve a copy of the restraint order on anyone affected by it (including the suspected offender). There may therefore be a tension between a desire to move quickly to prevent assets being transferred, removed, or dissipated, and a wish to avoid alerting the suspected offender to the existence of the investigation. For this reason, restraint orders are sometimes obtained only immediately prior to the arrest of the suspected offender and served on him at the time of his arrest.

The restraint order may require the suspected offender to provide information, but the material produced by him under this compulsion cannot be used in evidence at his trial.

Restraint orders are dealt with in more detail in chapter 2.

The offences charged

Decisions on investigation and charging are exclusively matters for the prosecution. However these decisions should not be driven by a desire to raise revenue from eventual confiscation proceedings[9].

Nevertheless, where a range of possible charges may equally appropriately be brought, from a proceeds of crime and confiscation point of view charges should be chosen and framed to cover as much as possible of the suspected offender's benefit from his criminal conduct (so maximising his benefit of particular criminal conduct on conviction) and to result in him having a criminal lifestyle[10] for confiscation purposes.

This will involve care in selecting the specific offence or offences charged (including, if appropriate, one or more of the criminal lifestyle offences listed within schedule 2), the number of offences charged (bearing in mind that where a person is convicted of more than three offences from each of which he has obtained a benefit that may trigger a finding of a

---

[9] See for example R (London Borough of Islington) v Bajaj [2020] EWCA Crim 1111

[10] s75

criminal lifestyle[11]), and the indictment period (which, if appropriate, should be a period of at least six months[12]).

Care should be taken where specimen offences are charged that they are sufficient not only to reflect the nature and seriousness of the alleged criminality, but also that they are sufficient from a confiscation point of view.

In relation to schedule 2 offences, where the alternative charges are otherwise equally appropriate, a money laundering charge under s327 or s328 is to be preferred to a charge under s329 (which is not a schedule 2 offence), a charge in relation to a brothel under s33 or s34 Sexual Offences Act 1956 is to be preferred to a charge under s33A of that Act (which is not a schedule 2 offence), and a cannabis charge under s4 Misuse of Drugs Act 1971 is to be preferred to a charge under s6 of that Act (which is not a schedule 2 offence).

Suspected offenders should not be charged with additional offences simply to generate an enhanced confiscation order, where such additional charges would not otherwise be appropriate. In particular, it will usually not be appropriate to charge a money laundering offence where the alleged money laundering does not go beyond that necessarily involved in the commission of a predicate offence of which the alleged offender is also charged[13] unless it is considered that the money laundering offence may be provable even where, ultimately, the defendant is acquitted of the predicate offence.

The timing of charging

Generally, for the purposes of confiscation, charging a suspected offender sooner rather than later will be beneficial. This is because, where a convicted defendant is found to have a criminal lifestyle, the statutory assumptions will apply to a period beginning on the 'relevant day'. The 'relevant day' is typically the first day of the period of six years which ends

---

[11] See s75(3)(a)

[12] See s75(2)(c) and *R v Panayi* [2019] EWCA Crim 413

[13] See for example *CPS Nottinghamshire v Rose* [2008] EWCA Crim 239

with the day on which the suspected offender was charged with the offence of which he is ultimately convicted and which forms the basis of the confiscation proceedings[14].

The exception to this is where the suspected offender is currently being prosecuted for another offence but has not yet been convicted of that. In this event there may, in very rare circumstances, be advantages from a confiscation perspective in delaying charging in the current investigation until after the suspected offender has been convicted of the other offence[15].

Multiple investigations or prosecutions of the same person

Particular care should be taken in pursuing confiscation proceedings where a convicted defendant is also subject to other ongoing investigations or prosecutions. It is important to avoid obtaining a confiscation order which does not cover the full extent of the defendant's benefit of all his criminal conduct to date, in circumstances where it is open to the court to employ the criminal lifestyle assumptions (whether or not those assumptions are actually relied upon).

The best course in these circumstances may be to delay the making of any confiscation order until the other investigations or prosecutions have reached their conclusion. This is because, once such a confiscation order has been made, the court may be precluded from bringing into account in subsequent confiscation proceedings additional benefit obtained by the convicted defendant prior to the day on which that confiscation order was made[16].

---

[14] s10(8) & (9) and s85(1) & (2)

[15] Because of the limitation in s75(3)(b) to the period before the latest proceedings were started, meaning that a conviction for another offence after the suspected offender has been charged in the current investigation will not count as one of the 'at least two separate occasions' referred to in that subsection.

[16] See *R v Chahal & Chahal* [2014] EWCA Crim 101

Charging connected persons

The normal charging criteria should be applied where consideration is given to, for example, charging the spouse or partner of the alleged offender with a money laundering offence. Such charging decisions should not be driven by a desire to pursue confiscation proceedings more effectively where there are jointly held assets.

Charging a company

The normal charging criteria should be applied where consideration is given to charging a company (whether solely or in addition to one or more individuals). Such charging decisions should not be driven by a desire to pursue confiscation proceedings more effectively where there are assets held by the company. However, it should not be overlooked that a company may be subject to confiscation in the same way as a natural person.

Confiscation following the conviction of a company will be especially effective where all of the following apply:

- The company has been engaged in criminal conduct from which it has obtained a benefit, or which includes a schedule 2 offence;

- One or more directors of the company have also been engaged in that criminal conduct[17];

- The company has also been engaged in some legitimate activities[18]; and

- The company holds assets of value.

---

[17] Which will assist in proving that the 'directing mind' of the company has been engaged in criminal conduct, where that is required for the conviction of the company itself

[18] Making piercing the corporate veil in confiscation proceedings against a director of the company more difficult

If a restraint order is to be obtained against a company, careful consideration should be given to limiting the restraint order to the company's fixed assets (such as land and buildings, plant and equipment, and vehicles) and excluding bank accounts, trading stocks and debtors – especially where the company is also engaged in legitimate activities. This may permit legitimate trading to continue whilst preventing the disposal of valuable fixed assets.

CHAPTER TWO

RESTRAINT

A restraint order may be sought under POCA 2002 as soon as a criminal investigation is commenced in England and Wales[19] and the sole purpose of the restraint order is to prevent dissipation of realisable property which may be used to satisfy a potential confiscation order. It may be made against a defendant, a person under investigation and/or any other individual holding realisable property.

It is important to bear in mind that applications for restraint orders are civil proceedings within the crown court and that it is the civil standard of the 'balance of probabilities' which applies.

Conditions for a restraint order

The prosecutor making the application will need to satisfy (on the balance of probabilities) one of five conditions[20] to enable a restraint order to be made against the defendant or alleged offender:

1. A criminal investigation has started in England and Wales and there are reasonable grounds to suspect that the alleged offender has benefited from an offence (if issued on this ground, a reporting order is mandatory)[21];

2. Criminal proceedings have been started but not concluded and there is reasonable cause to believe the defendant has benefited from his criminal conduct[22];

3. The prosecution has or will apply to reconsider a case in the light of fresh evidence where no confiscation order was made and there

---

[19] s41

[20] s40

[21] s41(7B)

[22] s40(3)

is reasonable cause to believe the defendant has benefited from his criminal conduct [23];

4. The prosecution has or will apply to make a new calculation of the defendant's benefit figure based on fresh evidence and there is reasonable cause to believe the court will find an increased benefit from his criminal conduct; or

5. The prosecution has or will apply to increase the amount required to be paid under a confiscation order when it appears that the defendant's current available amount exceeds that found at the time the confiscation order was made and there is reasonable cause to believe the court will increase the amount required to be paid.

Commencement of proceedings

Proceedings are commenced once a warrant or summons in respect of the offence is issued by a justice of the peace under s1 of the Magistrates' Court Act 1980, when a public prosecutor issues a written charge and requisition, when a person is charged with the offence after being taken into custody without a warrant, or when a bill of indictment is preferred in accordance with section 2(b) or 2(ba) of the Administration of Justice (Miscellaneous Provisions) Act 1933[24]. If more than one time is found under these requirements, the proceedings are regarded as commenced at the earliest of them.

Conclusion of proceedings

Where a confiscation order is made against a defendant, proceedings are not concluded for the purposes of Part 2, POCA 2002 until such time as the confiscation order has been fully satisfied (including accrued interest), discharged or quashed (and there is no further possibility of appealing the decision to quash the order).[25]

---

[23] s40(4)

[24] s85(1) & (2)

[25] s85(5)

Fresh evidence

Fresh evidence can include evidence to assist the court:

(i)   to reconsider making a confiscation order when no such order was made and the court has not proceeded under s6[26]; or

(ii)   to reconsider making a confiscation order when the court proceeded under s6 but concluded the defendant had obtained no benefit and so no such order was made, and there is new evidence that the defendant benefited from his or her criminal conduct;[27] or

(iii)   to make a confiscation order where a defendant absconds after conviction or committal;[28] or

(iv)   to make a confiscation order where a defendant absconded more than three months previously but was neither acquitted nor convicted in commenced criminal proceedings;[29] and

there is reasonable cause to believe that the defendant has benefited from his criminal conduct.

A restraint order can be made if the prosecutor has applied (or is likely to apply) to the crown court to reconsider the benefit figure in a confiscation order and there is reasonable cause to believe that the court will decide that the amount found under the new benefit calculation will exceed the amount previously found.[30]

A restraint order can be made if the prosecutor has applied (or is likely to apply) to reconsider the amount available to satisfy a confiscation order and there is reasonable cause to believe that the court will decide that the

---

[26] s19

[27] s20

[28] s27

[29] s28

[30] s21 & s21(3)

amount found under the new calculation of the available amount will exceed the amount previously found.[31]

Reasonable grounds to suspect and reasonable cause to believe

Unfortunately, the terms "reasonable grounds to suspect" and "reasonable cause to believe" are not defined in the legislation or confiscation case law. Although a belief must be rational and based on adequate supporting material, it does not demand evidence sufficient to prove the validity of the belief. Reasonable grounds to suspect do not require reasonable cause to believe, as a suspicion is less concrete than a belief.

Risk of dissipation

The prosecution must be able to show there is a real, as opposed to fanciful, risk that assets may be dissipated if a restraint order is not made.[32] Practitioners must be alive to the extent to which such a risk exists. In some cases, and particularly in cases involving allegations of dishonesty, the risk of dissipation will speak for itself and will not prove problematic.[33] However, where there has been a delay in applying for the restraint order and there is no evidence to show the defendant has dissipated assets in the meantime, despite having had every opportunity to do so, it falls upon both the prosecutor and the judge to explain how it can be said there is a real risk of dissipation in the future.[34]

The principal question for the court must always be whether the protection of a restraint order is necessary on the facts to ensure as far as possible that any confiscation order will be efficacious[35].

---

[31] s 22 & s22(8)

[32] *Re AJ & DJ* (Unreported, 9 December 1992, CA) LJ Glidewell

[33] *Jennings v CPS* [2005] EWCA Civ 746

[34] *Re B* [2008] EWCA 1374

[35] *Jennings v CPS* [2005] EWCA Civ 746 at [50]

Scope of persons subject to a restraint order

Restraint orders can apply to any individual, company or body holding assets in which the defendant has an interest. The court may make such order as it believes is appropriate for the purpose of ensuring that the restraint order is effective.[36] This can include a restriction or prohibition on the defendant's travel outside the United Kingdom.[37]

Where the restraint order is based on the first condition

Those served with a restraint order based on the first condition should consider carefully the terms of the restraint order as the court must include a reporting requirement which requires the applicant for the order to report to the court on the progress of the investigation at such times and in such manner as the order may specify.

The court must discharge the restraint order if proceedings for the offence are not started within a reasonable time.[38]

The court does have the power to decide that in the circumstances of the case, a reporting requirement should not be imposed, but the court must give reasons for its decision, and may at any time vary the order so as to include a reporting requirement. [39]

The extent of property restrained

Often the prosecutor will seek a restraint order over all the assets of the defendant or alleged offender particularly where the restraint order has been sought on the basis that a criminal investigation has been started but, as yet, no criminal proceedings have been started.

Even where criminal proceedings have been started, for example because the defendant has been charged with an offence from which it is believed he has benefited, the extent of his benefit is likely to be largely unknown.

---

[36] s41(7)

[37] s41(7D) & *R v Pritchard* [2017] EWCA Crim 1267

[38] s41(7B) (a) & (b)

[39] s41(7C)

That uncertainty is compounded where it appears that the defendant has a criminal lifestyle[40] and so his benefit for confiscation purposes will be his actual and assumed benefit from his general criminal conduct.

So that whilst in theory the amount of realisable property that can be restrained may be limited to the amount of the defendant's benefit, in practice the court will permit a prosecutor a considerable amount of latitude.

If the prosecutor is not alleging that the defendant has a criminal lifestyle, he may seek a restraint order limited to specific assets which have an aggregate value sufficient to cover the expected amount of the defendant's benefit from his particular criminal conduct.

Any person who holds assets jointly with the defendant may be specifically restrained from dealing with those jointly held assets.

The recipient of a tainted gift from the defendant may be restrained from dealing with any realisable property he holds up to the value of the gift.

See below with regard to a restraint order over the property of a company which is not itself a defendant or alleged offender.

Requirements for information

The prosecution often take the opportunity upon making a request for a restraint order to seek a provision of information order[41], requiring the defendant or a third party holding the defendant's realisable assets[42] to disclose the full extent of his realisable property. The order may also require the defendant to provide other information where that is believed to be appropriate for the purpose of ensuring that the restraint order is effective.

---

[40] As to which, see chapter 9

[41] s41(6) & (7)

[42] *Re D (Restraint Order: Non-Party)* The Times, 26 January, 1995.

The format for the provision of such information is a signed witness statement, verified by a statement of truth[43];

"this witness statement is true to the best of his knowledge and belief and that he made the statement knowing that, if it were tendered in evidence, he would be liable to prosecution if he wilfully stated in it anything which he knew to be false or did not believe to be true".

Information provided in response to a provision of information order may not be relied on in the criminal proceedings pre-conviction, to protect against self-incrimination. However, these statements must be drafted accurately and carefully, as post-conviction the provision of information statement may be relied on in the confiscation proceedings.

Any such statements may be, and typically are, annexed to the prosecutor's statement of information made under s16.

Procedure for drafting a restraint order

The responsibility for drafting the restraint order lies with the prosecutor. The witness statement and the draft restraint order must be lodged with the court in accordance with the Criminal Procedure Rules 2020.[44] The Criminal Procedure Rules permit that a restraint order may be made without notice to the defendant[45] if the application is urgent or if there are reasonable grounds to believe that giving notice would cause the dissipation of realisable property that is the subject of the application.

In practice, most applications for restraint will be made *ex parte*, but prosecutors must be careful to ensure that they comply with the duty of full and frank disclosure and inform the court of all material facts[46]. A

---

[43] Rule 33.7(2) CrimPR

[44] Rule 33.51 CrimPR

[45] As permitted by s.42(1)(b)

[46] The key principles surrounding the duty of full and frank disclosure can be found in *Brink's Mat Ltd v Elcombe* [1988] 1 WLR 1350

failure to do so can have serious consequences, including the possibility that the prosecution will be disqualified from maintaining an order[47].

Prosecutors should also be careful to ensure that a full note of the hearing is taken and provided to the defence[48].

Restraint orders can be made administratively but the court or defendant may request a hearing.

When cases arise that are of particular complexity, for example those involving complex issues regarding trusts, company law, insolvency law, property law or family law, prosecutors should liaise with the appropriate court's administrator to enable the hearing to take place before a judge with the necessary expertise, if possible.[49] In urgent cases, the judge initially dealing with the application may be invited to make the restraint order, with a short return date so that the matter can then be further considered by a judge with appropriate expertise.

Service of the restraint order

In practice the restraint order once made will need to be promptly served on the person, or persons, who are affected by it. The suspected offender will therefore become aware that he is the subject of a criminal investigation (if he was not aware of that previously). The timing of the application for a restraint order may be influenced by an operational requirement not to prematurely disclose this to the subject of an investigation.

Application for variation or discharge

An application to vary or discharge a restraint order may be made by any person affected by the order or by the person who applied for the order[50].

---

[47] *Jennings v CPS* [2006] 1 WLR 182 AT [64]

[48] *Interoute Telecommunications (UK) Ltd v Fashion Gossip Ltd,* The Times 10.11.99 (ChD)

[49] *Stanford International Bank v Serious Fraud Office* [2010] EWCA Civ 137

[50] s42(3) PoCA

An application by a person affected by the order must be in writing and may be supported by a witness statement and must be served on the crown court, the person who applied for the order and any person who is prohibited from dealing with realisable property by the restraint order [51].

An application by the person who applied for the order may be made without notice if the application is urgent or if there are reasonable grounds for believing that giving notice would cause the dissipation of realisable property which is the subject of the application. The particulars to be included in the application are set out in the Criminal Procedure Rules[52].

Variation by consent

A restraint order may be varied by consent. Where a variation is to be made by consent any party may apply to the court for the order in the terms agreed. The crown court may deal with such an application without a hearing. The order which is agreed must be signed by the legal representatives acting for each of the parties (or by a litigant in person)[53].

In practice it may be possible for the legal representatives of the defendant or alleged offender, or a third party affected by the order, to negotiate with the prosecutor to agree to a variation of the restraint order. For example, where a defendant appears to hold more than sufficient assets to cover any likely confiscation order it may be advantageous for the restraint order to be limited to assets which he would not want to deal with (such as land and buildings or investments) and to release more fluid assets (such as bank accounts currently in use day to day).

A practical problem may arise with the use of bank accounts however as the bank may be unwilling to allow the operation of a bank account which might hold suspected proceeds of crime, in view of the risk of possible money laundering. The defendant or suspected offender may

---

[51] Rule 33.53 CrimPR

[52] Rules 33.54 & 33.55 CrimPR

[53] Rule 33.42 CrimPR

therefore find that, notwithstanding the variation of the restraint order, his bank accounts remain frozen. This may be resolved by discussion with the bank and perhaps agreement to open a new 'clean' bank account for future use.

Reasonable living expenses

Although a restraint order must make provision for the defendant's reasonable living expenses from the restrained assets, it is inevitable that the prosecution will apply for only limited provision of living expenses. The prosecutor may seek a limit as low as £250 per week.

Any person affected by the order can apply for variation of the restraint order to allow for reasonable living expenses and to make provisions for individuals to carry on a trade, business or profession[54].

An application for an upward variation should indicate the new limit proposed, the specific reasons for the increased figure which is required (for example to allow mortgage payments to be made, or by reference to actual living expenditures typically incurred prior to the restraint order) and confirm that no other sources of funds are available to the subject of the restraint order to meet his reasonable living expenses. Where the subject of the restraint order has other persons financially dependent on him, details should be provided as part of the application for a variation.

Legal expenses

Restraint orders may be varied to cover reasonable legal expenses. However, they do not permit the payment from restrained funds of legal expenses incurred relating to the offences in relation to which the restraint order is sought[55].

Undue delay

Those acting for parties subject to the restraint order should note that the second, third, fourth or fifth conditions will not be satisfied if the court

---

[54] s42

[55] s41(4) & (5)

believes that either there has been undue delay in continuing the proceedings or that the prosecutor does not intend to proceed[56].

Detention and seizure of property

The restraint order can make provision for the continued detention of property seized or produced to the police under a relevant power. The relevant powers are:

- s47C; or

- s352; or

- Part 2 or 3 of the Police and Criminal Evidence Act 1984.

The detention provision in the restraint order must identify the property to be detained. This may be by itemising the property, or by a description of the class or classes of property, or the provision may be expressed to include all property covered by the restraint order. The provision can also relate to property that may be seized or produced in the future.

Repatriation of property

The court also has the power to make a repatriation order requiring a defendant to repatriate to England and Wales assets held overseas. This may be useful to the prosecution in securing funds held in overseas bank accounts which are vulnerable to dissipation.

A repatriation order should only be sought where the applicant believes the realisation of assets held overseas will be necessary to satisfy a confiscation order in the amount of the defendant's benefit.[57]

---

[56] s40(7) & (8)

[57] *DPP v Scarlett* [2000] 1 WLR 515

Breach of the restraint order

Failure to comply with court orders relating to restraint, receivership and/or provision of information can amount to contempt of court. This will be a civil contempt[58].

However a person who fails to comply with a restraint order may be at risk of criminal prosecution for attempting to pervert the course of justice.

Where the breach of the order involves the concealing, transfer to another person, or removal from England and Wales, of criminal property[59] there may be a risk of prosecution for a money laundering offence[60].

Monitoring

Both prosecutors and the defence should monitor the need for restraint, or continuing with restraint, throughout the investigation and criminal proceedings. Each case should be considered on its own merits.

Management Receivers

The court has the power to appoint[61] a management receiver to manage, control and preserve the value of the defendant's restrained assets[62].

When can a restraint order be discharged?

It is open to a defendant to apply for the discharge of a restraint order at any time prior to the making of a confiscation order. There are a wide variety of reasons which may justify an application to discharge. While it

---

[58] *OB v The Director of the Serious Fraud Office* [2012] EWCA Crim 67

[59] As defined by s340

[60] For example under s327

[61] s48

[62] s49

is not possible to provide a definitive list, the lack of full and frank disclosure during an *ex parte* application is a frequent ground[63].

Where a confiscation order has been made, a restraint order will not normally be discharged until the confiscation order has been satisfied.

Any variation to the restraint order that is required to facilitate the sale of the defendant's assets will be managed by the prosecutor in liaison with the defendant or his legal representatives.

---

[63] See *Windsor & Hare v CPS* [2011] EWCA 143 and *R v (Golfrate Property Management Ltd & Dr. Gulam Adam) v Southwark Crown Court & Commissioner for Police for the Metropolis* [2014] EWHC 840 (Admin)

CHAPTER THREE

TRIAL & PLEAS

For matters relating to the conduct of trials on indictment, reference should be made to the main texts on criminal evidence and procedure[64] and the Criminal Procedure Rules.

The following matters should, however, be considered in relation to POCA:

1) The client should, in appropriate cases, be advised at the outset of proceedings of the risk of a confiscation enquiry if they should choose to plead guilty or are convicted after trial.

2) If it is intended that any basis of plea shall limit a subsequent confiscation enquiry, this should be made expressly clear and must be expressly agreed between the parties[65]. If it is not expressly agreed, then the prosecution is unlikely to be bound by the basis of plea when conducting its enquiries into a defendant's benefit from criminal conduct. The following form of words is suggested as a starting point[66]:

It is agreed between the prosecution and the defence that the figure of £ [...] is, for all purposes and including any subsequent confiscation proceedings, the totality of the defendant's benefit from criminal conduct. It is agreed that the benefit figure for any subsequent confiscation proceedings will be limited to this amount.

3) Where there is voluminous financial evidence, or issues surrounding the true valuation of items such as jewellery or drugs,

---

[64] For example, Archbold

[65] See *R v Lazarus* [2005] 1 Cr App. R. (S) 98, *R v Bakewell* [2006] 2 Cr. App. R. (S.) 277 and *R v Benton* [2007] EWCA Crim 126 CA

[66] And should be varied and amended subject to the nature of the agreement that has been reached between the parties.

every effort should be made to reach a final and accurate figure within the context of the trial. There should be no hesitation in the instruction of an expert for this purpose, as a failure to properly deal with these issues at trial may substantially disadvantage a party in subsequent confiscation proceedings. It may also cause considerable professional embarrassment if it later transpires in confiscation proceedings that the valuations or amounts relied upon for the defendant's sentence were entirely inaccurate.

4) If a party is minded to make a concession in the trial, or for the purposes of sentence, no such concession should be made without first considering the impact it may have on the subsequent confiscation proceedings.

CHAPTER FOUR

LEGAL AID VERSUS PRIVATE REPRESENTATION

This chapter deals with the available funding for legal expenses in proceedings connected to POCA.

CRIMINAL LEGAL AID

Prosecutions for money laundering offences and post-conviction confiscation proceedings

An individual prosecuted for a money laundering offence is entitled to avail themselves of legal aid funding under the same scheme that applies to all criminal prosecutions. In order to qualify for legal aid, a defendant will be required to demonstrate that their income is sufficiently low to meet the criteria for means testing. A defendant with a household disposable income of £37,500[67] or more will be ineligible for legal aid to provide for advice and assistance in a Crown Court trial. Even if the disposable income is below this level, a defendant may still have to pay monthly contributions to the Legal Aid Agency ("LAA") to provide for his representation. For further details of the underlying statutory position, reference should be made to the Legal Aid, Sentencing and Punishment of Offenders Act 2012 ("**LASPO**").

If an individual avails themselves of legal aid funding, solicitors should ensure they advise their client of the risk that, if they are convicted, the LAA will seek to recover the totality of the funds claimed by their representatives under the legal aid scheme, and advise the client that their funding position should be kept under review. For example, a defendant may obtain a representation order having been charged with a single count of money laundering with a relatively low value and a straightforward factual background. If, however, the defendant is then

---

[67] This figure is accurate as at 1 November 2021

joined to a case of conspiracy to defraud and money launder with a value in excess of £1m with substantial pages of evidence, but ultimately convicted of a low value substantive count, the representation fee claimed by their lawyers could run to hundreds of thousands of pounds. The LAA will reserve the right to recover the totality of that fee from the defendant. In such circumstances the defendant may well have been better served by self-funding their defence, so that their costs liability was proportionate and clear. For an example of the issues that can arise, solicitors should refer to *R (On the application of the Director of Legal Aid Casework) v Crown Court at Southwark & Ian Swingland*[68].

Confiscation proceedings follow conviction, therefore, the defendant's representation will continue to be covered by the same legal aid order that was granted for his advice and representation in respect of the underlying prosecution.

If there has been a change of representative between the criminal trial and the confiscation proceedings, or if no representation has been in place prior to the confiscation, a defendant can apply to the court for a representation order. It should be borne in mind, however, that the fees available to counsel in confiscation proceedings are very limited: see Criminal Legal Aid (Remuneration) Regulations 2013, Schedule 1 para 14.

Enforcement Proceedings in the Magistrates' Court

These are considered fresh proceedings instigated by the prosecution. A defence team must apply for a fresh representation order, irrespective of whether they have previously represented the defendant in the Crown Court.

---

[68] *R (On the application of the Director of Legal Aid Casework) v Crown Court at Southwark & Ian Swingland*[68] [2021] EWHC 397 (Admin)

Applications for redetermination pursuant to s.22 and s.23 POCA

These constitute separate proceedings and should attract a separate payment under the legal aid scheme: *Regina v Mace*[69].

CIVIL LEGAL AID

Civil legal aid is available in order to deal with restraint orders (para 40(1)(a), Schedule 1 LASPO), but the provision of that funding is, again, subject to the applicant for funding meeting the necessary test in respect of means in form CIV MEANS 2. That said, in many cases the existence of a restraint order will severely restrict an individual's access to assets and, therefore, the means available to fund their case privately. That does not mean that the position in respect of Legal Aid funding will be straightforward, particularly if the restrained assets may be returned to the client in the event that an application for discharge or variation of the restraint order succeeds.

An application for civil legal aid must also meet the criteria on form CIV APP 1 regarding merits/prospects of success and the scope of the representation to be provided.

It is advisable that litigators consider all the aforementioned implications and aspects of representation in confiscation proceedings at an early stage of the proceedings, thereby enabling clients to make an informed decision as to whether they wish to have legal aid or private representation.

---

[69] *Regina v Mace*[69]. SCCO ref: 184/5

CHAPTER FIVE

THE FUNDAMENTALS OF CONFISCATION

This chapter provides a brief outline of the fundamentals of confiscation.

The eight questions to be addressed

In essence the court, before finalising a confiscation order against a defendant, has to address and resolve eight questions:

1) Does the court have power to make a confiscation order?

2) Does the defendant have a criminal lifestyle?

3) What is the amount of the defendant's benefit?

4) How much of the defendant's benefit was obtained jointly?

5) What is the defendant's available amount?

6) What amount should the defendant be required to pay?

7) How much time should the defendant be allowed to make payment?

8) How long should the default sentence be?

Does the court have power to make a confiscation order?

All confiscation orders are made in the crown court[70]. The court will have the power (and in most cases is obliged) to commence confiscation

---

[70] A proposal to give Magistrates' Courts power to make confiscation orders has never been implemented.

proceedings if the prosecutor asks the court to do so, or the court believes it is appropriate to do so[71], and the defendant has been either:

- Convicted of an offence in the current proceedings in the crown court; or

- Committed for sentence in the crown court in respect of an offence under any of the provisions of sections 14 to 20 of the sentencing code; or

- Committed to the crown court under s70 for a confiscation order to be considered[72].

In practice it is very rare for the court to instigate confiscation proceedings of its own volition. Confiscation proceedings are normally triggered by a request from the prosecutor.

The court may make a confiscation order following conviction, immediately before sentencing the defendant. Typically, however, the making of the confiscation order is postponed. Such a postponement must occur before sentencing and the court should (where no exceptional circumstances are found) commence the confiscation process (for example, by setting a timetable for the submission of any necessary statements under sections 16 to 18A and a deadline for the confiscation hearing) within 2 years of the date of conviction[73].

Does the defendant have a criminal lifestyle?

The answer to this question depends entirely upon the defendant's convictions – it has nothing to do with his actual lifestyle.

However, in order to fully resolve this question, the court may first have to determine whether the defendant has obtained aggregate benefit of at least £5,000 from offences for which he has been convicted together with

---

[71] s6(3)

[72] s6(2)

[73] s14

any offences which are being, or have been, taken into consideration in sentencing him.

Further details can be found in chapter 9 dealing with criminal lifestyle.

What is the amount of the defendant's benefit?

Where the court finds that the defendant does not have a criminal lifestyle, the amount of his benefit will be limited to the benefit of his particular criminal conduct. His particular criminal conduct is the conduct of which he has been convicted in the current proceedings and any offences being taken into consideration in sentencing in these proceedings[74].

Where the court finds that the defendant does have a criminal lifestyle, the amount of his benefit will be the actual and assumed benefit of his general criminal conduct. His general criminal conduct is all his criminal conduct (whenever this occurred) and includes any criminal conduct of his of which he has not been convicted[75].

The defendant's benefit of his general criminal conduct may therefore have three components:

a) The benefit of his particular criminal conduct;

b) The assumed benefit arising under the statutory assumptions[76]; and

c) Any other benefit arising from criminal conduct of his which is not being dealt with in sentencing in the current proceedings (including benefit arising in relation to criminal conduct of which he has previously been convicted, benefit of criminal conduct of which he has neither been convicted nor acquitted, and benefit which has been found by the court in previous confiscation proceedings against him – but subject to the

---

[74] s76(3)

[75] s76(2)

[76] See chapter 10 on the statutory assumptions

deduction of any amount previously ordered to be paid by him under a previous confiscation order)[77].

In practice prosecutors, and hence courts, typically ignore or overlook the third component.

The burden of proof falls generally upon the prosecution to satisfy the court, on a balance of probabilities[78], of the defendant's benefit. However, in relation to the statutory assumptions, although the burden falls initially on the prosecution, the burden then shifts to the defendant to show that an assumption is incorrect or that there would be a serious risk of injustice if an assumption were made[79].

Further details can be found in chapter 10 dealing with the statutory assumptions.

How much of the defendant's benefit was obtained jointly?

Where the court finds that the defendant obtained benefit jointly with one or more other persons, the whole of the benefit jointly obtained is treated as benefit of the defendant.

But the confiscation order should provide that it is not to be enforced to the extent that a sum has been recovered by way of satisfaction of a confiscation order made against another person in relation to the same jointly obtained benefit[80].

It is therefore necessary for the court to identify which benefit was jointly obtained and, if possible, with whom. Practitioners need to be mindful that they may need to remind the court of this fact.

---

[77] s8

[78] s6(7)

[79] s10(6)

[80] *R v Ahmad* [2014] UKSC 36

What is the defendant's available amount?

It is important to keep in mind that the exercise of determining the defendant's available amount is entirely separate from the consideration of his benefit.

The defendant's available amount is the aggregate of the total value of his interests in assets held by him (after taking into account any liabilities secured on those assets, such as outstanding mortgages) and the total value of any tainted gifts made by him – but subject to the deduction of obligations which have priority (as defined)[81].

Obligations having priority are very limited and, apart from outstanding fines, sums outstanding in respect of previous confiscation orders, and certain tax liabilities, are rarely encountered in practice.

When a confiscation order is being made the burden of proof falls generally upon the defendant to satisfy the court, on a balance of probabilities[82], as to his available amount[83].

What amount should the defendant be required to pay?

The defendant should be required to pay whichever is the lower of the amount of his benefit and his available amount, this is known as the recoverable amount[84].

However, if the court finds that it would be disproportionate to require the defendant to pay that amount, it should require him to pay the largest amount, not exceeding the recoverable amount, which would not be disproportionate[85].

A confiscation order simply requires the defendant to pay a specified sum or sums of money by a specified date or dates. The confiscation order

---

[81] s9

[82] s6(7)

[83] s7(2)

[84] s7 & s6(5)

[85] s6(5) and *R v Waya* [2012] UKSC 51

does not concern itself with how the defendant achieves that. So it does not, for example, require the defendant to sell any specified assets to enable him to make payment.

The court has additional powers which it may exercise with a view to ensuring payment is made[86] but these are not a necessary constituent of a confiscation order.

How much time should the defendant be allowed to make payment?

Unless the court allows further time to pay, the full amount required to be paid under a confiscation order must be paid on the day on which the order is made[87].

However, the court may allow a period, initially of no more than 3 months, for payment[88]. The court can set different dates for different parts of the total amount required to be paid.

The court may make an extension to the period initially allowed.

However, payment of the entire amount must be required by no later than 6 months after the day on which the confiscation order was made[89].

Where payment is made late, interest must be added to the amount outstanding under the confiscation order[90]. This interest is currently charged at a rate of 8% per annum.

It will be generally beneficial for a defendant to obtain an extension to the period initially allowed (and in many cases the court will in practice agree to this without difficulty) since – even where payment cannot be made within the 6 months – the extension will have the effect of reducing

---

[86] For example, compliance orders under s13A

[87] s11(1)

[88] s11(2) & (3)

[89] s11(4) & (5)

[90] s12

the interest arising on late payment. An application for an extension must be made before the existing deadline has passed[91].

How long should the default sentence be?

If the defendant fails to pay the full amount required to be paid, he may be committed to prison. A maximum sentence in default will be specified in the confiscation order.

The default sentence will be fixed by reference, amongst other factors, to the amount required to be paid under the confiscation order.

A table of maximum default sentences is set out in s35(2A).

The default sentence will be consecutive to any term of imprisonment for which the defendant has been sentenced for the offence.

See chapter 14 on the default sentence for further details.

---

[91] s11(4)

CHAPTER SIX

THE MEANINGS OF SOME COMMON TERMS

This chapter seeks to provide a user friendly explanation of the meanings of some common terms and expressions used in confiscation and restraint proceedings.

The defendant

The person who is, or is to become, the subject of the confiscation order is referred to as the defendant, even after he has been convicted. On occasion, for clarity, reference may alternatively be made to the subject as the 'convicted defendant' or the 'alleged offender'.

The defendant may be an individual or a company.

Confiscation proceedings do not simultaneously address more than one defendant. So, where there are a number of co-defendants, separate confiscation proceedings will be instituted against each defendant, resulting in separate confiscation orders against each of them.

Property

Property means an asset of any description[92], including tangible and intangible assets, money, and things in action. Property may be situated anywhere.

---

[92] s84(1)

Free property

Free property means any property except certain property which is subject to forfeiture, or a deprivation order, or is detained property under specified provisions[93].

Realisable property

Any free property held by the defendant, or held by the recipient of a tainted gift from the defendant, is realisable property[94].

So, where a person has received a tainted gift from a defendant, all his property (not just the property gifted to him) is realisable property.

The value of property

The basic rule is that the value of property is its current market value[95]. The market value means the open market value as between a willing buyer and a willing seller[96].

The market under consideration for this purpose is the market in which the person expected to sell the property in question.

This need not be a legitimate market. So, for example, where the property to be valued is an illegitimate holding of controlled drugs it will be necessary for the court to identify, on a balance of probabilities, whether those drugs were held for sale at street level, or for sale wholesale to another drug dealer. The basis of the valuation of those drugs will follow from that identification.

The value of the defendant's property for the purposes of confiscation is the value of his interest in it. Where the defendant and others have interests in an asset, the value of the defendant's interest in it is his proportion of the market value of the entire asset. There is no further

---

[93] s82

[94] s83

[95] s79

[96] *R v Islam* [2009] UKHL 30

reduction or discount to reflect the fact that the defendant owns only a part of the asset and therefore has restricted freedom to deal with it[97].

There may be additional considerations where the property to be valued is property obtained by the defendant by his criminal conduct or is property constituting a tainted gift[98].

Property obtained by a defendant

Property is obtained by a defendant if he obtains an interest in it[99]. In relation to land in England and Wales or Northern Ireland references to an interest are references to any legal estate or equitable interest or power[100]. In relation to property other than land, reference to an interest includes reference to a right (including a right to possession)[101].

A defendant "ordinarily obtains property if in law he owns it, whether alone or jointly, which will ordinarily connote a power of disposition or control, as where a person directs a payment or conveyance of property to someone else. He ordinarily obtains a pecuniary advantage if (among other things) he evades a liability to which he is personally subject"[102].

However, the converse is not necessarily the case, a person may have power to direct a payment or conveyance of property to someone else without having obtained the property in question[103].

Property held by a person

Property is held by a person if he holds an interest in it[104]. In relation to land in England and Wales or Northern Ireland references to an interest

---

[97] *R v Modjiri* [2010] EWCA Crim 829

[98] See below

[99] s84(2)(b)

[100] s84(2)(f)

[101] s84(2)(h)

[102] *R v May* [2008] UKHL 28

[103] *R v Seager and Blatch* [2009] EWCA Crim 1303

[104] s84(2)(a)

are references to any legal estate or equitable interest or power[105]. In relation to property other than land, reference to an interest includes reference to a right (including a right to possession)[106].

A person, such as a mere courier, may physically possess property without having a right to possession of it[107]. A mere courier, for example, does not hold (or obtain) the property of which he is in possession as courier.

In contrast, a thief of property does obtain a right to possession if it. The thief does therefore hold (and obtain) the property which he has stolen[108].

Restraint order

A restraint order is an order made in the crown court prohibiting a specified person or persons from dealing with the property specified in the order[109]. In effect, it freezes the assets in question with a view to their ultimately being available to satisfy an existing or future confiscation order[110].

See chapter 2 on restraint for further details.

Confiscation order

Strictly speaking, a confiscation order as defined in Part 2, POCA 2002 is limited to an order under s6 of that Act[111].

In this book however the term 'confiscation order' is used more widely to mean any order, whether under any part of POCA 2002 or predecessor

---

[105] s84(2)(f)

[106] s84(2)(h)

[107] *R v Allpress & others* [2009] EWCA Crim 8

[108] *CPS Nottinghamshire v Rose* [2008] EWCA Crim 239

[109] s41

[110] See chapter 2 on restraint

[111] s88(6)(a)

legislation, made by the court following the defendant's conviction[112], which requires him to pay a sum of money into court to disgorge the actual or assumed benefit obtained by him from his criminal conduct.

This therefore includes confiscation orders made under the Drug Trafficking Offences Act 1986, the Drug Trafficking Act 1994, and the Criminal Justice Act 1988 (and the corresponding provisions in Scotland and Northern Ireland).

A confiscation order is to be distinguished from a compensation order, which is an order requiring the defendant to pay a sum of money to compensate a victim of his criminal conduct[113].

Criminal lifestyle

A defendant does not have a criminal lifestyle unless he satisfies one or more of the statutory criteria, which are based entirely on the nature of, and benefit obtained by him from, offences of which he has been convicted or further offences taken into consideration in sentencing him.

Where a defendant has a criminal lifestyle that may have implications both for his benefit and his available amount.

In relation to his benefit, where he has a criminal lifestyle the confiscation order will reflect the benefit of his general criminal conduct. Where the defendant does not have a criminal lifestyle the confiscation order will reflect only the benefit of his particular criminal conduct.

In relation to his available amount, whether a defendant does, or does not, have a criminal lifestyle may affect the determination of whether any gifts made by him are tainted gifts.

See chapter 9 on criminal lifestyle for further details.

---

[112] And in some cases where he has absconded without being convicted

[113] Under chapter 2 of part 7 of the sentencing code

Benefit

The defendant's benefit of his criminal conduct is the value of the property obtained by him[114], solely or jointly[115], as a result of, or in connection with, that conduct[116].

Property obtained in connection with conduct does not extend to property lawfully purchased for value for the purpose of, but not otherwise in connection with, that conduct[117].

It is important to remember that the benefit is the value of property obtained – not property retained – by the defendant. So that, for example, a defendant found in illegitimate possession of controlled drugs will have the drugs seized from him but will nevertheless have obtained a benefit equal to the value of those drugs.

The benefit is not generally limited to the defendant's profit or gain from his criminal conduct. He is not permitted to deduct the costs he incurred in undertaking his criminal conduct from the value of the benefit obtained by him[118].

A confiscation order in the full amount of the defendant's benefit obtained would in many cases leave him in a worse financial position than he would have been in if he had not engaged in the criminal conduct at all, but a confiscation order is not limited to putting the defendant back in the position in which he would have been had he not committed his criminal conduct.

Benefit of particular criminal conduct

The defendant's benefit of his particular criminal conduct is the benefit of the conduct of which he has been convicted in the current proceedings

---

[114] *CPS v Jennings* [2008] UKHL 29

[115] *R v Ahmad* [2014] UKSC 36

[116] s76

[117] *R v James & Blackburn* [2011] EWCA Crim 2991

[118] *R v May* [2008] UKHL 28

and any offences being taken into consideration in sentencing in these proceedings[119].

Benefit of general criminal conduct

The defendant's benefit of his general criminal conduct is the actual and assumed benefit of all his criminal conduct (whenever this occurred) and includes any criminal conduct of his of which he has not been convicted[120].

The defendant's benefit of his general criminal conduct may therefore have three components:

a) The benefit of his particular criminal conduct;

b) The assumed benefit arising under the statutory assumptions[121]; and

c) Any other benefit arising from criminal conduct of his which is not being dealt with in sentencing in the current proceedings (including benefit arising in relation to criminal conduct of which he has previously been convicted, benefit of criminal conduct of which he has neither been convicted nor acquitted, and benefit which has been found by the court in previous confiscation proceedings against him – but subject to the deduction of any amount previously ordered to be paid by him under a previous confiscation order)[122].

Benefit of obtaining a pecuniary advantage by criminal conduct

Where a defendant obtains a pecuniary advantage as a result of, or in connection with, his criminal conduct, for example where he evades a tax

---

[119] s76(3)

[120] s76(2)

[121] See chapter 10 on the statutory assumptions

[122] s8

or duty for which he is personally liable, he obtains a benefit for confiscation purposes equal to the value of that pecuniary advantage[123].

The value of property obtained by the defendant's criminal conduct

POCA provides express rules for the valuation of property obtained by the defendant's criminal conduct[124].

The value, at the time the court makes its decision, of property obtained by the defendant's criminal conduct is the greater of :

a) the current value of the property obtained (if the defendant still holds it), and

b) the value of the property at the time the defendant obtained it, adjusted for subsequent changes in the value of money.

If the defendant no longer holds any part of the property obtained then, in substitution for (a) above, the current value of any property the defendant holds which directly or indirectly represents that property is valued.

If the defendant currently holds part but not all of the property obtained, then both the current value of the part of the property obtained which he still holds and the current value of any property the defendant holds which directly or indirectly represents the part which he no longer holds, are valued. The aggregate of these values is then used in substitution for (a) above.

If there is no property currently held by the defendant which directly or indirectly represents the property which he no longer holds, then that part of the computation cannot be completed. In these circumstances the only value open to the court will be that under (b) above and the property obtained will be valued on that basis.

---

[123] s76(5) & (7)

[124] s80

In practice it is commonplace for the prosecutor in a s16 statement to effectively ignore these somewhat complex provisions and value the benefit either (i) as simply the value of the property at the time the defendant obtained it, or (ii) as the value of the property at the time the defendant obtained it adjusted for subsequent changes in the value of money.

As the adoption of the more complex provisions can only serve to increase the defendant's benefit, and never to reduce it, this more pragmatic approach will not be challenged by the defendant.

The defendant's available amount

The defendant's available amount is the aggregate of the total value of his interests in assets held by him (after taking into account any liabilities secured on those assets, such as outstanding mortgages) and the total value of any tainted gifts made by him – but subject to the deduction of obligations which have priority (as defined)[125].

Obligations having priority are very limited and, apart from outstanding fines and certain tax liabilities, are rarely encountered in practice.

A gift

If the defendant transfers property to another person for no consideration, or for a consideration whose value is significantly less than the value of the property at the time of the transfer, this may be deemed a gift.

A gift will generally also have the following characteristics:

(i)   Transfer of legal and beneficial ownership of an asset

(ii) Acceptance of the gift by the donee, and

---

[125] s9

(iii) No intention on the part of the donor that the asset should be returned to him[126].

A tainted gift

Whether a gift is a tainted gift will in most cases depend solely on the date on which the gift was made.

If the court has determined that the defendant does not have a criminal lifestyle, a gift will be tainted if it was made after the date on which the offence was committed, or commenced to be committed (or the earliest such date, if the particular criminal conduct consists of more than one offence).

If the court has determined that the defendant does have a criminal lifestyle, or has not made a decision as to whether the defendant has a criminal lifestyle, then a gift will be a tainted gift if it meets one or both of the following criteria:

1. The gift was made after the first day of the period of six years ending with the day the proceedings were commenced against the defendant (or, if there are two or more offences and proceedings for them were started on different days, the earliest of those days); and/or

2. The gift was made at any time and was of property which was obtained by the defendant as a result of, or in connection with, his general criminal conduct or which represented in the defendant's hands property obtained by him as a result of or in connection with his general criminal conduct[127].

---

[126] *Re Somaia* [2017] EWHC 2554 (QB) at [76]

[127] s77

The significance of a tainted gift is that the value of it is a component in the defendant's available amount. A tainted gift does not of itself have any impact on the defendant's benefit[128].

The value of a tainted gift

PoCA 2002 provides express rules for the valuation of a tainted gift[129].

The value, at the time the court makes its decision, of a tainted gift is the greater of :

a) the current value of the property gifted (if the recipient of the gift still holds it), and

b) the value of the gift at the time it was given, adjusted for subsequent changes in the value of money.

If the recipient of the gift no longer holds any part of the property gifted then, in substitution for (a) above, the current value of any property the defendant holds which directly or indirectly represents that property is valued.

If the recipient of the gift currently holds part but not all of the gifted property, then both the current value of the part of the gifted property which he still holds and the current value of any property the recipient holds which directly or indirectly represents the part which he no longer holds, are valued. The aggregate of these values is then used in substitution for (a) above.

If there is no property currently held by the recipient of the gift which directly or indirectly represents gifted property which he no longer holds, then that part of the computation cannot be completed. In these

---

[128] In the case of *R v Johnson* [2016] EWCA Crim 10 it appears that the value of a tainted gift was treated by the prosecution as a component of the defendant's benefit, but it is not clear that the judge accepted that and, as the benefit figure was not the subject of the appeal, the point appears not to have been argued

[129] s81

circumstances the only value open to the court will be that under (b) above and the tainted gift will be valued on that basis.

Adjustments for changes in the value of money

In relation to the valuation of property obtained by the defendant from his criminal conduct, or property which constitutes a tainted gift, it may be necessary to make an adjustment for changes in the value of money.

The purpose of this is to effectively preserve the real value of the property obtained some time ago, in the face of a change in the value of the money being used to measure the value of that property. So that while the adjustment usually results in an increase in the number of pounds, this is intended merely to preserve (and not to increase) the real value of the amount concerned.

The adjustment is generally made using the CPIH index published monthly by the Office for National Statistics.

An example may help to make the process of adjustment clearer. At the time of writing the latest figure published for the CPIH index is that for the month of October 2021, which is 113.4.

Suppose we are dealing with property of £1,000.00 which was obtained on 19 March 2013. The CPIH index figure for March 2013 was 97.8. The £1,000.00 in March 2013 when adjusted for changes in the value of money becomes £1,159.51.

This has been calculated as

$$£1{,}000.00 \times \frac{113.4}{97.8} = £1{,}159.51$$

It might be said that in October 2021 one would need to have £1,159.51 to purchase the goods and services which could have been purchased for £1,000.00 in March 2013.

An obligation having priority

An obligation having priority is one which is to be deducted from the defendant's free property in the computation of his available amount[130].

Obligations which have priority are:

a) Outstanding fines and sums due under earlier confiscation orders made on conviction of an offence; and

b) Liabilities which would be included among the preferential debts[131] if the defendant were subject to bankruptcy proceedings.

Preferential debts include outstanding taxes in relation to which, broadly speaking, the defendant was collecting or holding monies on behalf of HMRC, such as PAYE deductions from his employees' remuneration and VAT collected from his customers.

Money laundering and confiscation

There are three principal money laundering offences.

The first is mere possession, use or acquisition of criminal property[132]. This is not a schedule 2 (criminal lifestyle) offence.

The second is entering into an arrangement which facilitates the acquisition, retention, use or control of criminal property by or on behalf of another person[133]. This offence might be considered the closest to money laundering in the traditional sense, since this offence focusses on money laundering with a view to securing an advantage for another person.

The third money laundering offence is concealing, disguising, converting, transferring, or removing from England and Wales, criminal

---

[130] s9(1)(a)

[131] See s386 Insolvency Act 1986

[132] s329

[133] s328

property[134]. This is perhaps the most commonly charged money laundering offence in practice.

The second and third money laundering offences are schedule 2 offences, conviction of which will necessarily involve a finding that the defendant has a criminal lifestyle for confiscation purposes.

A mere courier of money or property may not hold or obtain the property which he physically possesses. He may be guilty of the first type of money laundering offence. But he may not obtain for the purposes of confiscation the benefit of the money, or the value of the property, he possesses.

A money launderer who transfers money through the banking system, on the other hand, may be guilty of the second or third type of money laundering offence. He will, in the course of transferring money through the banking system, obtain for the purposes of confiscation the benefit of the money he transfers (whether or not he retains it)[135].

Piercing the corporate veil

A company has a legal existence and status which is separate from that of its shareholders and directors[136]. This is the case even where a company has only one shareholder who is also the sole director.

However, depending upon the facts and circumstances of the particular case, including the nature and extent of the criminality involved and the realities of the situation, "In the context of criminal cases the courts have identified at least three situations when a benefit obtained by a company may, depending on the facts, also be treated in law by POCA as a benefit obtained by the individual criminal"[137].

First if an offender attempts to shelter behind a corporate façade, or veil, to hide his crime and his benefits from it. Secondly, where an offender

---

[134] s327

[135] *Allpress and others v R* [2009] EWCA Crim 8

[136] *Salomon v A Salomon & Co Ltd* [1896] UKHL 1, [1897] AC 22

[137] *Boyle Transport (Northern Ireland) Ltd v R* [2016] EWCA Crim 19

does acts in the name of a company which (with the necessary *mens rea)* constitute a criminal offence which leads to the offender's conviction. Thirdly, where the transaction or business structures constitute a "device", "cloak" or "sham", i.e., an attempt to disguise the true nature of the transaction or structure so as to deceive third parties or the courts[138].

The courts have recognised the principles of concealment (where one or more companies have been interposed to conceal the identity of the real actors) and evasion (where there is a legal right against the person in control of the company which exists independently of the company's involvement and the company has been interposed so that the separate legal personality of the company will defeat the right or frustrate its enforcement)[139].

Strictly speaking, the concealment principle does not involve piercing the corporate veil at all, it simply involves recognising the true identities of the real actors which are initially concealed by the interposition of the company.

In practice, where a company carries on some legitimate trading in its own right it will often not be appropriate for the corporate veil to be pierced in confiscation proceedings against a director of, and/or shareholder in, the company.

The recoverable amount

The recoverable amount is the lower of the amount of the defendant's benefit and his available amount.

A hidden asset

Where the defendant is unable to satisfy the court, on the balance of probabilities, that his available amount is less than his benefit and is limited to identified assets of his, then the court may make a confiscation

---

[138] *R v Seager and Blatch* [2009] EWCA Crim 1303

[139] *Prest v Petrodel Resources Ltd and others* [2013] UKSC 34

order requiring him to pay an amount (not exceeding his benefit) which is higher than the value of those identified assets[140].

In these circumstances the situation is sometimes described as the court having made a finding that the defendant has hidden assets. However, the expression hidden assets is not found in POCA and there is no statutory basis for it.

The court should base its conclusions concerning the defendant's available amount on a just and proportionate view of the facts as a whole, which may enable a defendant to satisfy the evidential burden on him, even when his own evidence proves to be an untruthful and unreliable or even non-existent as to the source, nature, and extent of his current assets[141].

Disproportionality

Following the decision of the UK Supreme Court in R v Waya[142], and based on Article 1 of the First Protocol to the European Convention on Human Rights, section 6 was amended to add the phrase "only if, or to the extent that, it would not be disproportionate to require the defendant to pay the recoverable amount," to the provision requiring a confiscation order to be made in the recoverable amount.

A confiscation order is intended to require the defendant to disgorge the benefit obtained by him from his criminal conduct. Where the court finds that he has already disgorged benefit, it would be disproportionate to require him to disgorge that benefit a second time by way of confiscation. So, the rule against disproportionality has the flavour of addressing potential double recovery.

A confiscation order will be disproportionate if it requires the defendant to pay an amount representing the benefit of property obtained by him which has already been returned, or is sure to be returned, intact to the

---

[140] s7

[141] *McIntosh and Marsden v R* [2011] EWCA Crim 1501

[142] *R v Waya* [2012] UKSC 51

loser. This could occur where items or monies were stolen but have been returned to the victim, or where money has been fraudulently borrowed but is sure to be repaid.

Similarly, where Value Added Tax has been obtained from customers in trading tainted by illegality and that VAT has been accounted for to HMRC by the defendant, it would be disproportionate to require the defendant to pay those monies over a second time by way of confiscation[143].

However, a confiscation order will not be disproportionate simply because it causes hardship, or is for a large amount, or it requires several defendants each to pay a sum which has been obtained successively by each of them, or it requires the defendant to pay the whole of a sum which he obtained jointly with others (although there will be a restriction on the amount he is required to pay where the value of jointly obtained benefit has already been recovered from another person with whom it was jointly obtained[144]), or it requires a defendant to pay the whole of a sum which he has obtained by crime without enabling him to set off the expenses incurred in committing the crime.

A confiscation order based on the value of a tainted gift, which had subsequently lost its value, was not held to be disproportionate, although the confiscation order might cause hardship[145].

The amount ordered to be paid

The defendant will be required to pay the recoverable amount, which is the lower of the amount of the defendant's benefit and his available amount, unless it would be disproportionate to require him to pay that amount. In that event, the confiscation order should require him to pay

---

[143] *R v Harvey* [2015] UKSC 73

[144] *R v Ahmad* [2014] UKSC 36

[145] *R v Johnson* [2016] EWCA Crim 10

the largest amount, not exceeding the recoverable amount, which would not be disproportionate[146].

Default sentence

If the defendant fails to pay the full amount required to be paid, he may be committed to prison. A maximum sentence in default will be specified in the confiscation order.

The default sentence will be fixed by reference, amongst other factors, to the amount required to be paid under the confiscation order.

A table of maximum default sentences is set out in s35(2A).

The default sentence will be consecutive to any term of imprisonment for which the defendant has been sentenced for the offence.

See chapter 14 on the default sentence for further details.

---

[146] s6(5)

CHAPTER SEVEN

THE SECTION 18 & SECTION 18A QUESTIONNAIRES

Introduction

Where a court is proceeding, or considering proceeding, towards making a confiscation order under section 6 it may make an order under section 18 requiring the defendant to supply information to the court. In practice the section 18 order will be drafted by the prosecutor before being formally issued by the court.

There are no express limits in section 18 or in the Criminal Procedure Rules, on the type or amount of information which may be required by the order. Therefore, the questions may be wide-ranging and sweeping in nature. The purpose of the information requested will be relevant, or potentially relevant, to the quantification of the defendant's benefit or available amount or to the making of the confiscation order.

The order may require the information to be provided in a specified manner and by a specified date[147].

For the purposes of illustration, and to assist practitioners, an example of a completed s18 questionnaire is produced at Appendix 1. This illustrative questionnaire is intended to be representative of ones the authors have typically encountered, it is not a model of best practice.

Some of the ground covered in the s18 questionnaire may already have been covered in a request for information as an element in a restraint order previously obtained in respect of the defendant (and possibly other persons)[148] or information obtained under other investigation powers[149].

---

[147] s18(3)

[148] Under s41(7)

[149] For example under Part 8, POCA 2002

Practitioners should ensure that clients are reminded of the contents of request for information documentation, before instructions are taken on the section 18 questionnaire.

Below is a table of information which typically may be requested within a section 18 questionnaire where it is believed that the defendant does **NOT** have a criminal lifestyle for confiscation purposes.

Defendant's full name, date of birth, national insurance number and current address		
Names and dates of birth of the defendant's spouse / domestic partner and dependants		
Defendant's current sources of income and State Benefits received		
Details of property (land and buildings) currently owned solely or jointly by the defendant		
Details of motor vehicles currently owned solely or jointly by the defendant		
Details of bank accounts currently held by the defendant, solely or jointly		
Details of accounts or investments with other financial institutions currently held by the defendant, solely or jointly		

Details of premium bonds, national savings certificates and other national savings products currently held by the defendant, solely or jointly		
Details of cash currently held by the defendant, solely or jointly		
Details of credit card accounts or cryptocurrency accounts currently held by the defendant, solely or jointly		
Details of any shares, bonds, securities, unit trusts, share or currency options, or futures currently held by the defendant, solely or jointly		
Details of any security or safety deposit boxes, or assets held in storage facilities to which the defendant has access		
Details of any insurance policies, pension policies or entitlements, annuity policies or similar investments currently held, solely or jointly, which have or may acquire a surrender or transfer value		
Details of any company of which the defendant is a director or in which he holds an interest in more than 5% of the issued share capital		
Details of any business in which the defendant is a partner or in which he holds an interest in more than 5% of the business assets or profits		

Details of bank accounts or accounts or investments with other financial institutions or properties or other assets which the defendant does not hold, either solely or jointly, but in which he has a legal or beneficial interest		
Details of any trusts of which the defendant is a beneficiary, or potential beneficiary, or trustee		
Details of any other assets currently held by the defendant, solely or jointly, or in which he has a legal or beneficial interest, not disclosed above		
Details of any civil proceedings against the defendant in relation to the criminal conduct of which he has been convicted		
Details of any mortgages or charges on land and buildings disclosed above		
Details of any other secured or preferential liabilities		
Details of any outstanding fines or amounts outstanding in respect of any confiscation orders against the defendant		
Details of any gifts made by the defendant, or assets transferred by him at significantly less than open market value, at any time since the commencement of the criminal conduct of which he has now been convicted		

Below is a Table of information which typically may be requested within a s18 questionnaire where it is believed that the defendant **does** have a criminal lifestyle for confiscation purposes.

Note: In the following paragraphs the 'relevant day' means [*date*]		
Defendant's full name, date of birth, national insurance number and current address		
Names and dates of birth of the defendant's spouse / domestic partner and dependants		
Defendant's sources of income and State Benefits received since the relevant day		
Details of property (land and buildings) owned solely or jointly by the defendant at any time since the relevant day, and of the purchases and sales of those properties		
Details of motor vehicles owned solely or jointly by the defendant at any time since the relevant day, and of the purchases and sales of those motor vehicles		
Details of bank accounts held by the defendant, solely or jointly at any time since the relevant day		
Details of accounts or investments with other financial institutions held by the defendant, solely or jointly at any time since the relevant day		

Details of premium bonds, national savings certificates and other national savings products held by the defendant, solely or jointly at any time since the relevant day		
Details of cash currently held by the defendant, solely or jointly		
Details of credit card accounts or cryptocurrency accounts held by the defendant, solely or jointly at any time since the relevant day		
Details of any shares, bonds, securities, unit trusts, share or currency options, or futures held by the defendant, solely or jointly at any time since the relevant day		
Details of any security or safety deposit boxes, or assets held in storage facilities to which the defendant has had access at any time since the relevant day		
Details of any insurance policies, pension policies or entitlements, annuity policies or similar investments held, solely or jointly, at any time since the relevant day which have or may acquire a surrender or transfer value		
Details of any company of which the defendant is or was a director or in which he holds or held an interest in more than 5% of the issued share capital at any time since the relevant day		

Details of any business in which the defendant is or was a partner or in which he holds or held an interest in more than 5% of the business assets or profits at any time since the relevant day		
Details of bank accounts or accounts or investments with other financial institutions or properties or other assets which the defendant does not hold, either solely or jointly, but in which he has had a legal or beneficial interest at any time since the relevant day		
Details of any trusts of which the defendant is or was a beneficiary, or potential beneficiary, or trustee at any time since the relevant day		
Details of any other assets held by the defendant, solely or jointly, or in which he has or had a legal or beneficial interest at any time since the relevant day, not disclosed above		
Details of any civil proceedings against the defendant in relation to criminal conduct of which he has been convicted		
Details of any mortgages or charges on land and buildings disclosed above		
Details of any other secured or preferential liabilities		

Details of any outstanding fines or amounts outstanding in respect of any confiscation orders against the defendant		
Details of any gifts made by the defendant, or assets transferred by him at significantly less than open market value, at any time since the commencement of any criminal conduct of which he has been convicted, or (if earlier) at any time since the relevant day		

Use of the information provided by the defendant

The information supplied by the defendant in response to the s18 questionnaire will be used by the prosecutor, along with other information, in the preparation of his section 16(3) or section 16(5) statement.

However, no information, given in response to a section 18 order, that the defendant has benefited from criminal conduct is admissible in evidence in proceedings for any offence.[150]

The significance of the prosecutor accepting an allegation in the defendant's s18 response

Where the prosecutor accepts an allegation made in the defendant's section 18 response, or in any other statement to the court relevant to the defendant's available amount or to a section 10A determination of the defendant's interest in any property, then the court may treat that as conclusive of the matter to which it relates.[151]

---

[150] s18(9)

[151] s18(6)

The significance of failing to respond to matters in the section 18 questionnaire

If the defendant, without reasonable excuse, fails to comply with a section 18 order the court may draw such inferences as it believes to be appropriate.[152] A failure to respond to the section 18 order may also be considered to be contempt of court.

The implications of false, inaccurate, or incomplete responses to the s18 questionnaire

Where the defendant's responses to the section 18 questionnaire can be shown to be false, inaccurate or incomplete the prosecutor may infer that little weight should be given to evidence from the defendant in the confiscation proceedings and the court may be invited to infer that the defendant has 'hidden' assets.

The defendant and his legal advisers should therefore take care that, as far as possible, the defendant's responses are accurate and complete. Where it is not possible to provide accurate and complete information it is advisable to indicate the difficulties which the defendant faces in responding fully to the questionnaire.

It should not be forgotten that the prosecutor has access to information from other sources including credit reference agencies, HM Revenue and Customs, the Benefits Agency, local authorities, the Land Registry, the Driver and Vehicle Licensing Centre, the National Crime Agency, evidence and unused material from the trial, responses to production orders and other orders under Part 8 POCA 2002, and open-source information. The defendant therefore faces serious risk of adverse consequences in the confiscation proceedings if he withholds or provides misleading information in his response to the s18 questionnaire.

The section 18A order

Where a court is proceeding, or considering proceeding, towards making a confiscation order under s6 and is considering whether to make a

---

[152] s18(4)

formal determination under s10A of the extent of the defendant's interest in any property, it may make an order under s18A requiring an '*interested person*' to supply information to the court. In practice, the section 18A order will be drafted by the prosecutor before being issued by the court.

An '*interested person*' in this context means a person, other than the defendant, whom the court thinks is, or may be, a person holding an interest in property in which the defendant also has an interest[153].

There are no express limits in section 18A, or in the Criminal Procedure Rules, on the type or amount of information which may be required by the order, except that the purpose of obtaining the information must be to help the court carry out its functions under section 10A. In practice the information requested should be relevant, or potentially relevant, to the quantification of the defendant's available amount.

The order may require the information to be provided in a specified manner and by a specified date[154].

Use of the information provided by the interested person

The information supplied by the interested person in response to the s18A questionnaire will be used by the court when considering whether to make a determination under s10A and in making that determination.

However, no information, given in response to a s18A order, by the interested person is admissible in evidence in proceedings against that person for any offence.[155]

The significance of the prosecutor accepting an allegation in the interested person's s18A response

Where the prosecutor accepts an allegation made in the interested person's s18A response, or in any other statement to the court relevant

---

[153] s18A(1)

[154] s18A(3)

[155] s18A(9)

to the s10A determination, then the court may treat that as conclusive of the matter to which it relates.[156]

The significance of failing to respond to matters in the s18A questionnaire

If the interested person, without reasonable excuse, fails to comply with a s18A order the court may draw such inferences as it believes to be appropriate.[157] A failure to respond to the s18A order may also be considered to be contempt of court.

---

[156] s18A(6)

[157] s18A(4)

CHAPTER EIGHT

THE SECTION 16 STATEMENT OF INFORMATION

The s16(3) statement (where it is asserted that the defendant has a 'criminal lifestyle'), or s16(5) statement (where the prosecutor does not believe the defendant has a 'criminal lifestyle'), will typically have been prepared by an accredited financial investigator acting as a member of the prosecution team.

The statement will set out the prosecution assertions regarding the defendant's benefit and available amount, along with background details and other information. This is a key document in the confiscation process. Appended to the statement will be documents which the author considers relevant to put before the court in the confiscation proceedings.

As the proceedings progress toward the confiscation hearing the prosecution may submit further statements, under s16(6), adding to or modifying the assertions in the first statement in the light of information or explanations provided by, or on behalf of, the defendant or additional information received from other sources, or simply on a reconsideration of the position by the prosecution.

The following table indicates matters which may usefully be addressed within a prosecutor's s16(3) or s16(5) statement.

Items relevant only to criminal lifestyle cases, s16(3), are in *italics*.

Items relevant only to non – criminal lifestyle cases, s16(5), are underlined.

	Append	Statute/Rule
Cover sheet, defendant, preparer, date, presenter		CrimPR 33.13 (5)(a) & (b)
Introduction		
Whether criminal lifestyle		s6(4), s75
If criminal lifestyle then reason		*s16(3)(a) & CrimPR 33.13 (5)(d)(i)*
Information on any relevant civil proceedings		s6(6)
Summary of offence(s) of which convicted	Indictment or summons	CrimPR 33.13 (5)(c)
Date of commencement of offences of which convicted		s77(5)
Date of commencement of proceedings		s85(1)
Date of conviction		s10(10)
Relevant basis of plea (if any)	Basis of plea	
Relevant sentencing remarks and / or prosecution opening (if any)	Sentencing remarks and / or prosecution opening	

Court's confiscation timetable		
Section 18 information request order to defendant & response	s18 questionnaire & response	s18
Any section 18A information request order to third party & response	s18A questionnaire & response	s18A
Personal history, date of birth, address, spouse / partner, dependants		
Defendant's known legitimate income, State Benefits, employments, business interests & taxes paid	HMRC witness statement	
If CL case, previous convictions, benefit of previous convictions, previous confiscation orders, amount ordered to be paid under previous confiscation orders	*Pre-cons, previous confiscation orders & variations, JARD database record*	*s76(2), s8*
Restraint order & any variations	Restraint order, witness statement, variations	
Benefit of particular criminal conduct	Relevant trial documents	s76(3)
Valuations of benefit of particular criminal conduct, drugs etc	Relevant valuers' statements	
Change in value of money uplift re benefit of particular criminal conduct	Computation & CPIH index table	s80(2)(a)

If CL, figures of benefit of previous convictions, previous confiscation orders, less amount ordered to be paid under previous confiscation orders		*s76(2), s8*
If CL, change in value of money uplift re benefit of previous convictions, previous confiscation orders	*Computation & CPIH index table*	*s80(2)(a)*
If CL, assumed benefit of general criminal conduct		*s10*
If CL, 'relevant day' & reason for it		*s10(8) & (9)*
If CL, any reason why the court should not make a statutory assumption		*s16(4) & CrimPR 33.13 (5)(d)(iv)*
If CL, assumed benefit of property transferred to defendant after relevant day	*Bank statements & spreadsheets relied upon*	*s10(2)*
If CL, change in value of money uplift re assumed benefit of property transferred to defendant	*Computation & CPIH index table*	*s80(2)(a)*
If CL, assumed benefit of property held by defendant after date of conviction	*Ownership documents & valuations relied upon, mortgage statements*	*s10(3)*

If CL, change in value of money uplift re assumed benefit of property held by defendant (on items where benefit based on value when first obtained)	*Computation & CPIH index table*	*s80(2)(a)*
If CL, assumed benefit of expenditure incurred by defendant after relevant day	*Documents evidencing expenditure*	*s10(2)*
If CL, change in value of money uplift re assumed benefit of expenditure incurred by defendant	*Computation & CPIH index table*	*s80(2)(a)*

Summary table of benefit		
Information on benefit obtained jointly		
Available amount – assets & secured liabilities	Relevant documents of ownership, valuations, secured liabilities	s9(1)(a)
<u>**If NOT CL, details of gifts made since commencement of offences of which convicted**</u>	<u>Relevant documents</u>	<u>s9(1)(b), s77(5)</u>
If CL, details of gifts made since 'relevant day'	*Relevant documents*	*s9(1)(b), s77(2) & (9)*
If CL, and any offences preceded 'relevant day', details of gifts made since those offences AND evidence that property gifted was, or represented, benefit of defendant's general criminal conduct	*Relevant documents*	*s9(1)(b), s77(3)*

Valuations of tainted gifts at time gift made, uplifted for changes in the value of money	Valuations and uplift computation	s81
Current valuations of property comprised in tainted gifts	Valuations	s81
Any appropriate reduction re outstanding fines or amounts required to be paid under confiscation orders following earlier convictions	Previous court orders, JARD database record	s9(2)(a)
Any appropriate reduction re preferential debts	Documents evidencing the debts	s9(2)(b)
Evidence, if any, suggesting hidden assets		s7
Evidence, if any, relevant to a determination the court may make regarding the defendant's interest in any property likely to be realised or used to satisfy the confiscation order		s16(6A) & s10A, CrimPR 33.13 (5)(f)
Summary of available amount		s9
Summary of recoverable amount		s7
Proportionality – summary of proposed amount ordered to be paid		s6(5)
Effect on court's other powers		s13
Request for compliance order, if any, and reasons for it		s13A, CrimPR 33.14 (3)(b)

Address for defendant's response to the s16 statement		s17
Explanation of significance of defendant's acceptance of any allegation or failure to respond to a s17 order		s17(2) & (3), CrimPR 33.13 (7)
Certificate under Regulation 11 of the Criminal Justice and Data Protection (Protocol No 36) Regulations 2014		
Note regarding time to pay		s11
Note regarding default sentence		s35(2A)

The format of the s16 statement

It may assist the parties and the court if the s16 statement is split into separate documents as follows

- Concise pleadings as to the matters upon which the prosecutor relies

- Statements and any exhibits upon which the prosecutor relies, and

- If required, a skeleton argument.

This may assist in ensuring that evidence, submissions and the factual basis on which the case is put are readily discernible. This format was provisionally proposed by the Law Commission in its consultation paper on confiscation[158].

---

[158] Law Commission consultation paper 249, Confiscation of the proceeds of crime after conviction, September 2020

It may be appropriate for the s16 statement to be reviewed by a lawyer with appropriate qualifications and experience before being issued.

A s16 statement is a 'statement of information' provided to the court and not a written witness statement in the sense of s9 Criminal Justice Act 1967 or Rule 33.7 of the Criminal Procedure Rules. The s16 statement is not required to include a statement of truth[159].

For the purposes of illustration, and to assist practitioners, an example of a s16 statement of information in a relatively simple factual situation is produced at Appendix 2. This illustrative s16 statement is intended to be representative of ones the authors have typically encountered, it is not a model of best practice.

The difference between trial, sentencing and confiscation

At trial the focus will be on whether the defendant's guilt is proved to the criminal standard. At sentencing the focus may be on harm done by the offending of which the defendant has been convicted, and on mitigation. Confiscation is different.

In confiscation the focus will be on the benefit obtained by the defendant from his criminal conduct, and on his available amount. The burden of proof is on a balance of probabilities[160].

In the confiscation proceedings:

- The judge, counsel and witnesses may not have been involved in the previous trial or sentencing;

- The scope of the hearing will be wider than issues raised at the previous trial or sentencing;

- Only one defendant is the subject of a confiscation order, whereas a count at trial may apply to more than one defendant;

---

[159] s9(2)(b) Criminal Justice Act 1967 refers

[160] s6(7)

- Evidence inadmissible at trial may be introduced[161].

The first question for the court

The first question for the court[162] is whether the defendant has a 'criminal lifestyle' as defined[163]. In order to resolve that it will sometimes be necessary for the court to have reached conclusions as to the benefit obtained by the defendant from the offences of which he has been convicted (and other offences taken into consideration on sentencing for those offences) and the length of time over which the defendant was engaged in the criminal conduct of which he has been convicted. See chapter 9 on criminal lifestyle.

If the defendant does not have a criminal lifestyle and has not obtained any benefit from any of the offences of which he has been convicted in the current proceedings (and other offences taken into consideration on sentencing for those offences), then the court should not go on to make a confiscation order[164].

The benefit of the defendant's particular criminal conduct

The benefit of the defendant's particular criminal conduct as defined[165] is the value of the property obtained by him[166] as a result of or in connection with that criminal conduct[167].

The criminal conduct is that relating to the offences of which the defendant has been convicted in these proceedings (including offences taken into consideration in sentencing). In establishing the extent of those offences the court will examine the wording of the summons or

---

[161] *Clipston v R [2011] EWCA Crim 446*

[162] s6(4)(a)

[163] s75

[164] This follows from s6(5). The defendant will have no benefit on which to base a confiscation order.

[165] s76(3)

[166] *CPS v Jennings [2008] UKHL 29*

[167] s76(4) & (7)

indictment, and may look at any accompanying statement of facts and the underlying legislation, to identify the case which the defendant was called upon to meet. Where, for example, proceedings have been conducted on the basis that the counts charged are accepted to be specimen counts, the benefit of particular criminal conduct may be calculated on that basis[168].

However, the words "in connection with" should not be interpreted too broadly[169]. Whilst the costs of committing a crime are not deductible expenses in computing the benefit of that crime, those costs are not themselves benefit obtained in connection with that crime, even though the costs may have been incurred for the purpose of the crime.

Reference in the s16 statement to the sentencing remarks at trial, or the prosecution opening note, may assist the court in identifying the criminal conduct and relevant facts found at trial, and hence in the determination of the defendant's benefit of particular criminal conduct.

Where a basis of plea has been accepted by the prosecution (and that acceptance has not been limited to the purpose of sentencing) then the benefit found in confiscation must not be inconsistent with that basis of plea[170].

The burden of proving the benefit of the defendant's particular criminal conduct on a balance of probabilities falls upon the prosecution.

If a defendant obtains a pecuniary advantage as a result of or in connection with conduct, he is to be taken to obtain a sum of money equal to the value of that advantage[171].

A defendant "ordinarily obtains property if in law he owns it, whether alone or jointly, which will ordinarily connote a power of disposition or

---

[168] *R v Panayi [2019] EWCA Crim 413; R (London Borough of Haringey) v Roth [2020] EWCA Crim 967; London Borough of Barnet v Kamyab [2021] EWCA Crim 543*

[169] *James & Blackburn v R [2011] EWCA Crim 2991; Ahmad & Ahmed v R [2012] EWCA Crim 391*

[170] *R v Lunnon [2004] EWCA Crim 1125; R v Lazarus [2004] EWCA Crim 2297*

[171] s76(5)

control, as where a person directs a payment or conveyance of property to someone else. He ordinarily obtains a pecuniary advantage if (among other things) he evades a liability to which he is personally subject"[172].

A defendant does not obtain a criminal benefit from criminal conduct of which he has been formally acquitted[173].

The benefit of the defendant's general criminal conduct

The initial burden of proving the benefit of the defendant's general criminal conduct on a balance of probabilities falls upon the prosecution. Where the statutory assumptions[174] are employed this is not a high hurdle. "Once a criminal lifestyle has been established, it falls to the prosecution, if it can, to prove, on the balance of probabilities, that the defendant has obtained property. The prosecution, as the first three assumptions in s10 indicate, may do so by proving that property has been transferred to the defendant, that he has obtained property, or that he has incurred expenditure after the relevant day"[175].

The burden then shifts to the defendant to rebut the assumption in respect of an item of property by "clear and cogent evidence"[176] or to show that there would be a serious risk of injustice if the assumption were made[177]. "As to the weight that has to be given to the word 'serious', any real as opposed to a fanciful risk of injustice can be appropriately described as serious"[178].

Chapter 9 deals with the determination of whether the defendant has a criminal lifestyle and chapter 10 with the operation of the statutory assumptions when he does.

---

[172] *R v May [2008] UKHL 28*

[173] *R v Briggs-Price [2009] UKHL 19*

[174] s10

[175] *Whittington v R [2009] EWCA Crim 1641*

[176] *R v Singh [2008] EWCA Crim 243*

[177] s10(6)(b)

[178] *R v Benjafield & others [2000] EWCA Crim 86*

Benefit obtained jointly

Where property forming part of the defendant's benefit has been obtained jointly with one or more other persons "the confiscation order should be made for the whole value of the benefit thus obtained, but should provide that it is not to be enforced to the extent that a sum has been recovered by way of satisfaction of another confiscation order made in relation to the same benefit"[179].

Benefit obtained in a conspiracy

Where the defendant has been convicted of a conspiracy offence it is important in the confiscation proceedings to have regard only to the role played by this defendant in the conspiracy and the benefit obtained, solely or jointly, by him.

The position was summarised by the Court of Appeal in *Rooney*[180] –

"In short, the position is, as we understand it:

(a) if a benefit is shown to be obtained jointly by conspirators, then all are liable for the whole of the benefit jointly obtained.

(b) If, however, it is not established that the total benefit was jointly received, but it is established that there was a certain sum by way of benefit which was divided between conspirators, yet there is no evidence on how it was divided, then the court making the confiscation order is entitled to make an equal division as to benefit obtained between all conspirators.

(c) However, if the court is satisfied on the evidence that a particular conspirator did not benefit at all or only to a specific amount, then it should find that is the benefit that he has obtained".

---

[179] *R v Ahmad [2014] UKSC 36*

[180] *R v Rooney [2010] EWCA Crim 2*

Available amount

The defendant's available amount is the aggregate of the total of the values (at the time the confiscation order is made) of all the free property[181] then held by the defendant (whether acquired legitimately or illegitimately) minus the total amount payable in pursuance of obligations which then have priority (such as outstanding fines or sums remaining outstanding under earlier confiscation orders, and debts which would be preferential in a bankruptcy) and the total values (at the time the confiscation order is made) of all tainted gifts made by the defendant[182].

Available amount – burden of proof

The burden rests upon the defendant to show, on a balance of probabilities, that his available amount is less than his benefit[183]. In practice however the s16 statement will normally include information which the prosecutor holds concerning the defendant's available amount.

In a straightforward situation, "once the benefit has been proved, it is permissible and ought normally to be the approach of the court, to conclude that the benefit remains available until the defendant proves otherwise"[184].

However even where the defendant is found not to have told the truth about his realisable assets "there is no principle that a court is bound to reject a defendant's case that his current realisable assets are less than the full amount of the benefit, merely because it concludes that the defendant has not revealed their true extent or value, or has not participated in any revelation at all . . . Other sources of evidence, apart from the defendant himself, and a view of the case as a whole, may persuade a court that the

---

[181] s82

[182] s9

[183] s7(2)

[184] *R v Barwick [2000] EWCA Crim 3551*, a case involving thefts of money by a single defendant, in which no statutory assumptions applied

assets available to the defendant are less than the full value of the benefit"[185].

For example, where the defendant's benefit includes the full amount of a benefit obtained jointly with others, or drugs or other property which has been seized or forfeit, or assumed benefit in relation to which there is no remaining realisable property, then the defendant's benefit will not translate into an equivalent available amount.

Available amount – property in which others have an interest

Where the defendant and one or more others have an interest in property, for example because it is owned jointly or where a liability is secured upon it, only the value of the defendant's interest is to be taken into account in arriving at his available amount.

Available amount – gifts made by the defendant

Where the defendant has made a gift the issue of whether that was a tainted gift will generally be determined solely by the date on which was the gift was made[186].

A transfer made for consideration will be a 'gift' for this purpose if the consideration for the property was significantly less than the value of that property at the time of the transfer[187].

However, case law suggests that for there to be a gift there must be (i) transfer of legal and beneficial ownership in an asset, (ii) acceptance of the gift by the donee, and (iii) no intention on the part of the donor that the asset should be returned to him[188].

Where a defendant does not have a criminal lifestyle, a tainted gift is any gift made at any time after the date (or earliest date) on which the offence or offences of which he has been convicted (or are taken into account in

---

[185] *McIntosh & Marsden v R [2011] EWCA Crim 1501*

[186] s77

[187] s78(1)

[188] *Re Somaia [2017] EWHC 2554 (QB)*

sentencing) in the current proceedings, were committed or commenced to be committed[189].

Where a defendant does have a criminal lifestyle, a tainted gift is any gift made at any time after the 'relevant day'. The 'relevant day' here means the first day of the period of six years ending on the day (or the earliest day) on which proceedings for the offence concerned were started against the defendant[190]. The 'relevant day' for the purpose of tainted gifts will be the same as the 'relevant day' for the purposes of the statutory assumptions, except where the operation of s10(9) causes the 'relevant day' for the statutory assumptions to be a more recent date.

Where the defendant does have a criminal lifestyle, any gift is also tainted if it was made by the defendant at any time and was of property which was obtained by him as a result of, or in connection, with his general criminal conduct or which (in whole or in part and whether directly or indirectly) represented in the defendant's hands property which was obtained by him as a result of, or in connection with, his general criminal conduct[191].

Valuations

Where property is to be valued the basic rule is that its value is the market value[192]. That means the price which a willing seller would accept from a willing buyer operating in the market in which the defendant expected to sell the property[193]. That is not necessarily a legitimate market.

---

[189] s77(5), (6) and (7)

[190] s77(2), (3) and (9)

[191] s77(3)

[192] s79(2)

[193] *R v Islam [2009] UKHL 30*

Valuation of property obtained by conduct

When valuing property obtained by conduct, the value of the property at the time the court makes its decision is the greater of the value produced under the next two paragraphs[194].

Firstly, the court will consider the value of the property at the time the person obtained it, adjusted to take account of later changes in the value of money. This adjustment is usually made using the CPIH inflation index published monthly by the Office for National Statistics.

Secondly, if the person still holds the property obtained, the court will consider the current value of that property. If the person holds no part of that property, the court will consider the current value of any property which directly or indirectly represents it in his hands. If the person holds part (but not all) of that property, the court will consider the current value of that part and any property which directly or indirectly represents the other part in his hands.

Valuation of a tainted gift

When valuing a tainted gift, the value of the property at the time the court makes its decision is the greater of the value produced under the next two paragraphs[195].

Firstly, the court will consider the value at the time of the gift of the property given, adjusted to take account of later changes in the value of money. This adjustment is usually made using the CPIH inflation index published monthly by the Office for National Statistics.

Secondly, if the recipient still holds the property given, the court will consider the current value of that property. If the recipient holds no part of that property, the court will consider the current value of any property which directly or indirectly represents it in his hands. If the recipient holds part (but not all) of that property, the court will consider the

---

[194] s80

[195] s81

current value of that part and any property which directly or indirectly represents the other part in his hands.

Piercing the corporate veil

Whether the corporate veil of a company may be pierced, so that benefit obtained by the company is obtained by the individual and property held by the company is held by the individual, will depend upon the facts of the case. In particular the court should have regard to the realities of the matter and the nature and extent of the criminality involved[196].

Recoverable amount

The recoverable amount will be the amount of the defendant's benefit, unless the defendant shows his available amount is less than his benefit – in which case the recoverable amount will be equal to his available amount (or a nominal amount if his available amount is nil)[197].

The amount ordered to be paid

The amount ordered to be paid will be the recoverable amount, unless it would be disproportionate to require the defendant to pay that amount – in which case the amount ordered to be paid will be equal to the largest amount which would not be disproportionate[198].

---

[196] *Boyle Transport (Northern Ireland) Ltd v R [2016] EWCA Crim 19*

[197] s7

[198] s6(5)

CHAPTER NINE

CRIMINAL LIFESTYLE

Does the defendant have a criminal lifestyle?

The first question for the court[199] is whether the defendant has a 'criminal lifestyle' as defined[200]. In many cases it will be a straightforward matter to conclude that the defendant has a criminal lifestyle.

However in some cases in order to resolve that it will be necessary for the court to have reached conclusions as to the benefit obtained by the defendant from the offences of which he has been convicted (and other offences taken into consideration on sentencing for those offences) and the length of time over which the defendant was engaged in the criminal conduct of which he has been convicted.

The expression 'criminal lifestyle' may be misunderstood by some defendants, as it has nothing to do with the defendant's 'lifestyle' in the everyday sense of that word.

A defendant has a criminal lifestyle if, and only if, he satisfies one of the tests in s75[201].

Schedule 2 offences

Where a defendant has been convicted of an offence listed in Schedule 2 he will inevitably have a criminal lifestyle[202].

In these circumstances it is not necessary for the defendant to have obtained any benefit from the offence. For example, conviction for a failed attempt to import a controlled drug would result in the defendant

---

[199] s6(4)(a)

[200] s75

[201] s75(1)

[202] s75(2)(a)

having a criminal lifestyle even where no controlled drug or other benefit had been obtained.

Care should be taken to confirm that the precise offence of which the defendant has been convicted is listed in Schedule 2. Offences which are not listed in Schedule 2, but are sometimes mistaken to be (because they have some similarities to offences which are included in the schedule), include

- acquisition, use or possession of criminal property, contrary to s329

- cultivation of a cannabis plant, contrary to s6 Misuse of Drugs Act 1971

- keeping a brothel used for prostitution, contrary to s33A Sexual Offences Act 1956.

A defendant convicted of one of these offences may nevertheless have a criminal lifestyle if one or more of the other tests in s75 are met.

The significance of benefit in determining criminal lifestyle

Where a defendant has not been convicted of a Schedule 2 offence he will not have a criminal lifestyle where he has not obtained any benefit from the offences of which he has been convicted.

Where a defendant (who has not been convicted of a Schedule 2 offence) has obtained a benefit from one or more offences of which he has been convicted, but the aggregate of his 'relevant benefit' is less than £5,000, he will not have a criminal lifestyle[203].

What constitutes his 'relevant benefit' depends upon the circumstances.

---

[203] s75(4)

Other routes to a criminal lifestyle

Aside from having been convicted of a Schedule 2 offence, there are three key routes to a finding that a defendant has a criminal lifestyle.

Offence committed over a period of at least six months

Where the defendant has been convicted of an offence which he has committed over a period of at least six months from which he has benefited, and his 'relevant benefit' is not less than £5,000, he will have a criminal lifestyle[204].

Here his 'relevant benefit' means the aggregate of his benefit from the conduct which constitutes the offence and his benefit from conduct which constitutes an offence which has been or will be taken into consideration by the court in sentencing the defendant for the offence[205].

The period over which he has committed the offence depends upon the facts. It is not determined simply by the dates set out in the indictment or summons.

Where one or more co-defendants are convicted it is necessary for the court to consider each defendant's conduct individually in determining whether he has committed the offence over a period of at least six months and whether he has obtained a 'relevant benefit' of at least £5,000[206].

Defendant convicted in the same proceedings of four or more offences

Where the defendant has been convicted in the same proceedings of four or more offences, from each of which he has benefited, and his 'relevant benefit' is not less than £5,000, he will have a criminal lifestyle[207].

Here his 'relevant benefit' means the aggregate of his benefit from the conduct which constitutes the offences of which he has been convicted

---

[204] s75(2)(c) and (4)

[205] s75(6)

[206] *R v Bajwa & others [2011] EWCA Crim 1093*

[207] s75(2)(b), (3)(a) and (4)

in the current proceedings and his benefit from conduct which constitutes an offence which has been or will be taken into consideration by the court in sentencing the defendant for these offences[208].

For this purpose, an offence of which the defendant has been convicted in the current proceedings, but from which he has obtained no benefit, is disregarded.

Defendant having earlier been convicted on two separate occasions

Where the defendant has been convicted in the current proceedings of one or more offences from which he has benefited, and in the period of six years ending with the day when these proceedings were started[209] (or, if there is more than one such day, the earliest day) he was convicted on at least two separate occasions of an offence constituting conduct from which he has benefited, and his 'relevant benefit' is not less than £5,000, he will have a criminal lifestyle[210].

Here his 'relevant benefit' means the aggregate of his benefit from the conduct which constitutes the offences of which he has been convicted in the current proceedings, and his benefit obtained from the offences of which he was convicted in the six-year period referred to above, and his benefit from conduct which constitutes an offence which has been or will be taken into consideration by the court in sentencing the defendant for any of these offences[211].

For this purpose, any conviction of an offence of which the defendant has been convicted outside the current proceedings but after the date on which the current proceedings started, is disregarded.

---

[208] s75(5)

[209] As defined by s85(1) and (2)

[210] s75(2)(b), (3)(b) and (4)

[211] s75(5)

Changes in the value of money

When considering whether the 'relevant benefit' is not less than £5,000[212] it may be necessary to take account of changes in the value of money[213].

It is possible that at the time the benefit was obtained the value of it was less than £5,000 but that, as a result of subsequent changes in the value of money, at the time the court makes its decision as to whether the defendant has a criminal lifestyle the sterling value of that benefit, uplifted for changes in the value of money, will be greater than, or equal to, £5,000.

The importance of charging

The number and wording of the charges of which the defendant is convicted can have an impact upon whether the defendant has a criminal lifestyle.

For example, Emily is an accountant who on two occasions, on 4 February 2020 and on 23 September 2020, dishonestly submitted false documents to her employer resulting on each occasion in her being paid £3,000 to which she was not entitled. Emily has no previous convictions. If Emily is charged with, and convicted of, fraud by abuse of position between 4 February 2020 and 23 September 2020, she will have a criminal lifestyle (having been convicted of an offence committed over a period of at least six months from which she has benefited by not less than £5,000).

On the other hand, if Emily is charged with, and convicted of, two separate counts of fraud by abuse of position, the first on 4 February 2020 and the second on 23 September 2020, she will not have a criminal lifestyle (as she does not satisfy any of the tests in s75).

---

[212] s75(4)

[213] s80(2)(a)

The significance of a criminal lifestyle – benefit

Where a defendant does not have a criminal lifestyle his benefit for the purposes of confiscation is limited to the benefit of his particular criminal conduct. That is his benefit of the offences of which he has been convicted in the current proceedings and any benefit of offences taken into consideration in sentencing in the current proceedings.

Where a defendant does have a criminal lifestyle his benefit for the purposes of confiscation is his benefit of his general criminal conduct. That is his actual and assumed benefit of all his criminal conduct (whether or not he has been convicted of it). That includes his benefit of all earlier convictions (subject to a deduction in respect of amounts which he has been ordered to pay under previous confiscation orders) and assumed benefit arising under the statutory assumptions[214].

The significance of a criminal lifestyle – available amount

A defendant's available amount includes (appropriately valued) the value of any tainted gifts he has made. However the definition of what constitutes a tainted gift varies depending upon whether or not the defendant has a criminal lifestyle.

Where a defendant does not have a criminal lifestyle, a tainted gift is any gift (which for this purpose includes a transfer for a consideration which is significantly less than the value of the property transferred at the time of the transfer) made at any time after the date (or earliest date) on which the offence or offences of which he has been convicted (or are taken into account in sentencing) in the current proceedings, were committed or commenced to be committed[215].

Where a defendant does have a criminal lifestyle, a tainted gift is any gift (which for this purpose includes a transfer for a consideration which is significantly less than the value of the property transferred at the time of the transfer) made at any time after the 'relevant day'. The 'relevant day' here means the first day of the period of six years ending on the day (or

---

[214] s10

[215] s77(5), (6) and (7)

the earliest day) on which proceedings for the offence concerned were started against the defendant[216].

Where the defendant does have a criminal lifestyle, any gift (which for this purpose includes a transfer for a consideration which is significantly less than the value of the property transferred at the time of the transfer) is also tainted if it was made by the defendant at any time and was of property which was obtained by him as a result of, or in connection with, his general criminal conduct or which (in whole or in part and whether directly or indirectly) represented in the defendant's hands property which was obtained by him as a result of, or in connection with, his general criminal conduct[217].

---

[216] s77(2), (3) and (9)

[217] s77(3)

CHAPTER TEN

THE STATUTORY ASSUMPTIONS

When do the statutory assumptions operate?

If, and only if, the defendant has a criminal lifestyle the court must make the four statutory assumptions for the purpose of deciding his benefit from general criminal conduct[218].

The first assumption (concerning property transferred to the defendant) and the third assumption (concerning expenditure incurred by the defendant) relate to the period after the 'relevant day'.

The second assumption (concerning property held by the defendant) relates to the period after the date of conviction. If there are two or more offences and the convictions are on different dates, the date of conviction for this purpose is the date of the latest[219].

None of the statutory assumptions apply to any period after the date on which the confiscation order is made. Subject to that, the fourth assumption (relating to other interests in property) applies at any time.

In practice, when preparing a s16 statement, the prosecutor will apply the statutory assumptions for a period ending on a convenient date (such as the date of the most recent bank statement in his possession).

When are the statutory assumptions not made?

The court must not make a required assumption in relation to an item of property or expenditure where the assumption is shown (on a balance

---

[218] s10(1)

[219] s10(10)

of probabilities[220]) to be wrong, or there would be a serious risk of injustice if the assumption were made[221].

Note that the statute refers to a serious risk of injustice, not a risk of serious injustice. In that connection, "As to the weight that has to be given to the word "serious", any real as opposed to a fanciful risk of injustice can be appropriately described as serious. The court, at the end of the confiscation process, has therefore a responsibility not to make a confiscation which could create injustice"[222].

However, the statute does not afford the court a general discretion as to whether to make the statutory assumptions, for example on grounds of hardship to the defendant.

If the court does not make one or more of the required assumptions it must state its reasons[223].

The 'relevant day'

The 'relevant day' for the purposes of the first and third assumptions is normally the first day of the period of six years ending on the day on which proceedings for the 'offence concerned' were started. Where there are two or more offences which satisfy the condition of s6(2)[224] as being the 'offence concerned' and proceedings for these offences were started on different days, then the 'relevant day' is based on the earliest of these days[225].

The rules for determining the date on which proceedings for an offence are started are set out in s85(1) and (2). Typically proceedings are started when the defendant is charged with the offence or when a summons or

---

[220] s6(7)

[221] s10(6)

[222] *R v Benjafield and others [2000] EWCA Crim 86*

[223] s10(7)

[224] See s6(9)

[225] s10(8)

warrant is issued. If more than one date is found in relation to proceedings, they are started on the earliest of them.

For example, Stuart was charged with an offence on 1 November 2020. Stuart has never previously been subject to confiscation. The 'relevant day' will be 2 November 2014. The first and third statutory assumptions will therefore apply to the period beginning on 3 November 2014 (the first day after the 'relevant day') and ending on the day on which the confiscation order is made against Stuart.

However, the normal rule is modified to avoid overlapping periods where the defendant has previously been subject to a confiscation order in which statutory assumptions applied (or could have been applied[226]). Where such a previous confiscation order has been made against the defendant the 'relevant day' in the current proceedings cannot be earlier than the date of that previous criminal lifestyle confiscation order (or if there is more than one, the latest one)[227].

For example, Terrence was charged with an offence on 1 November 2020. Terrence has previously been subject to a confiscation order on the basis of a criminal lifestyle. That confiscation order was made on 15 June 2016. The 'relevant day' therefore cannot be 2 November 2014, it will instead be 15 June 2016. The first and third statutory assumptions will therefore apply to the period beginning on 16 June 2016 (the first day after the 'relevant day') and ending on the day on which the new confiscation order is made against Terrence. In this way there is no overlapping period in which the assumptions can apply in both confiscation proceedings.

Fresh charges

Where a defendant, having been initially summoned or charged with one or more offences, is subsequently charged with different offences, care must be taken to correctly identify each 'offence concerned' which satisfies the criteria of s6(2), i.e., an offence for which the defendant is

---

[226] *R v Chahal and Chahal [2014] EWCA Crim 101*

[227] s10(9)(a)

being sentenced in the Crown Court. Consideration can then be given to the date on which proceedings for each 'offence concerned' were started, so that the correct 'relevant day' can be determined.

The first assumption – property transferred to the defendant

The first statutory assumption is that any property transferred to the defendant after the relevant day was obtained by him as a result of his general criminal conduct (and is therefore benefit of his) and at the earliest time he appears to have held it[228].

Typically this assumption is applied to monies transferred to, or deposited in, bank accounts (and accounts with other financial institutions) which are held in the name of the defendant.

Where an account is held jointly by the defendant and another, then each joint holder is deemed to hold the entirety of the funds in the account. Accordingly, the entirety of a sum deposited in the account will be property transferred to the defendant and be assumed benefit of his general criminal conduct.

Where the prosecutor can evidence, for example by the production of a bank statement, a credit of monies to an account held, solely or jointly, in the name of the defendant that will ordinarily be sufficient to discharge the initial burden of proof on the prosecutor and trigger the statutory assumption.

The burden then shifts to the defendant to show, on the balance of probabilities, that the assumption is incorrect (e.g., by showing that the funds were obtained legitimately or that the credit did not result in property being transferred to the defendant) or that there would be a serious risk of injustice if the assumption were made.

In many cases the narrative on the bank statement can assist in identifying the source of a bank credit.

---

[228] s10(2)

Where a bank credit arises from a transfer from one of the defendant's bank accounts to another account of his then it does not result in property being transferred to the defendant (as the funds were his property before the transfer) and so no assumed benefit arises.

Where there is a pattern of periodic credits of similar amounts (for example on the same day every week or every month) this may indicate the credits arise from a recurring source of income, such as a weekly wage or monthly rent receipt. Examination of the pattern of credits to the defendant's bank accounts may therefore yield useful corroborative evidence of the sources of those credits.

Where cash is drawn from one bank account and cash is banked in another that may indicate that effectively what has occurred is simply a transfer from one account to another. That evidence is particularly strong where the cash withdrawal and the cash banking are of the same amount and on the same day.

A better understanding of the defendant's financial affairs will be achieved where transaction data from all of his bank accounts is brought together in a single schedule and that transaction data is than analysed into different types of incomes and expenditures (such as wages, motoring costs, transfers between accounts, etc.) and summarised. Use of appropriate computer software will greatly assist in this process.

Information from HMRC

The prosecutor may obtain information from HMRC, typically in the form of a witness statement and supporting exhibit, setting out information held by HMRC regarding the defendant's income from employment or self-employment.

This information should be treated with care, particularly in the case of income from self-employment or rental receipts. The figures produced by HMRC may be amounts of net income – but the credits to the defendant's bank accounts will be gross receipts (and may also include amounts of output VAT charged by him). Self-employed income may be for an accounting period which differs from the tax year (for example, the self-employed income for a year to 30 September 2019 may be taxable in the income tax year to 5 April 2020).

As a result the information from HMRC may not correctly identify the amounts and dates of relevant credits to the defendant's bank accounts.

It may be appropriate for a forensic accountant to be instructed where the criminal lifestyle assumptions are applied.

Bank accounts not in the name of the defendant

Where a bank account is held not in the name of a defendant (being held, for example, in the name of a spouse or a limited company) the burden rests upon the prosecution to show that credits to the account represent property transferred to the defendant.

See, for example, the cases of *Gor*[229] (bank account in the name of a spouse) and *Boyle Transport (Northern Ireland) Ltd*[230] (piercing the corporate veil).

The risk of duplication

There is a risk of duplication of benefit where the defendant has been engaged in particular criminal conduct which has generated monies which have been banked. The defendant's benefit of the offences of which he has been convicted will be included in his benefit of particular criminal conduct, but when the proceeds are banked those monies may be included again as his assumed benefit of general criminal conduct.

If it can be demonstrated that those monies are from his particular criminal conduct then there would be a serious risk of injustice if they were included again in his total benefit, and they should therefore be excluded.

---

[229] *Gor v R [2017] EWCA Crim 3*

[230] *Boyle Transport (Northern Ireland) Ltd v R [2016] EWCA Crim 19*

However, the burden will rest on the defendant to satisfy the court that there is indeed a duplication.

In the case of *Priestley*[231] the defendant had sold perfume and champagne bearing counterfeit trademarks of well-known brands. He did not give evidence in his confiscation proceedings and was made subject to a confiscation order in excess of £2 million. He appealed. It was not disputed that the defendant had sold 218,334 bottles of perfume (which at £5 per bottle would produce £1,091,670) and that he had banked substantial sums of cash. The Court of Appeal found that the burden was on the defendant to demonstrate that applying the statutory assumption to the cash banked involved a duplication of benefit. The Crown Court judge was entitled to conclude on the evidence before him (or the lack of evidence) that there was no serious risk of injustice in applying the statutory assumption to the cash banked in addition to the defendant's benefit of particular criminal conduct.

The second assumption – property held by the defendant

The second statutory assumption is that any property held by the defendant after the date of his conviction was obtained by him as a result of his general criminal conduct (and is therefore benefit of his) and at the earliest time he appears to have held it[232].

The assumption can apply irrespective of the date on which the property in question was first held by the defendant.

Where the prosecutor can evidence, for example by the production of a Land Registry document or a vehicle registration document, property held in the name of the defendant that will ordinarily be sufficient to discharge the initial burden of proof on the prosecutor and trigger the statutory assumption.

Where others also have an interest in the property, the assumption applies to the defendant's interest in the property (but the burden will be on the

---

[231] *Priestley v R [2004] EWCA Crim 2237*, a case under the statutory assumptions of Criminal Justice Act 1988

[232] s10(3)

defendant to show that he did not obtain the property free of any other interests in it[233]).

The assumed benefit will be based on the greater of (a) the current value of the property, and (b) the value of the property when the defendant obtained it adjusted to take account of later changes in the value of money[234]. The value is the open market value at the relevant time[235].

On the face of it therefore whatever assets are identified as forming part of the defendant's available amount will also form part of his assumed benefit of general criminal conduct (where the defendant has a criminal lifestyle) except to the extent that the defendant can demonstrate that the property was acquired legitimately.

However, where credits to a bank account have already been considered in relation to the first assumption, the inclusion of the current balance on that bank account under the second assumption would involve a duplication of benefit and a serious risk of injustice. For that reason, balances on bank accounts are not normally included under the second assumption.

It may be appropriate to obtain an independent professional valuation of valuable property.

The third assumption – expenditure incurred by the defendant

The third statutory assumption is that any expenditure incurred by the defendant after the relevant day was met from property obtained by him as a result of his general criminal conduct[236] (and that therefore he has an equivalent assumed benefit of his general criminal conduct).

Where however the expenditure has been funded from a known source, such as a bank account which has already been considered in relation to the first assumption, the inclusion of the expenditure under this

---

[233] s10(5)

[234] s80

[235] s79

[236] s10(4)

assumption would involve a duplication of benefit and a serious risk of injustice. For that reason, expenditures from known sources are not normally included under the third assumption.

Indeed, it is common in s16 statements for the prosecutor to disavow any assertion of assumed benefit arising under the third assumption because of the risk of duplication.

Where there has been cash expenditure, which is considered to point to assumed benefit, it is appropriate to search for sources of that cash (such as cash withdrawals from known bank accounts or cash generated from particular criminal conduct). Where the source of the cash can be identified that may indicate that there would duplication, and hence a serious risk of injustice, if the assumption were to be applied to that expenditure.

Where the prosecutor can evidence expenditure, for example by a receipted invoice addressed to the defendant, that will ordinarily be sufficient to discharge the initial burden of proof on the prosecutor and trigger the statutory assumption.

Caution should be exercised in asserting general living expenditure based, for example, on household expenditure surveys from the Office for National Statistics. Every household is unique and average spending may not properly reflect the actual spending in the defendant's household. Also, such spending may be funded in part, for example, by bank expenditure from known bank accounts, cash drawn from known bank accounts and contributions by other members of the household.

The fourth assumption – interests held by others

The fourth statutory assumption is that, for the purpose of valuing any property obtained (or assumed to have been obtained) by the defendant, he obtained it free of any other interests in it[237].

---

[237] s10(5)

This assumption, unlike the first three statutory assumptions, does not directly result in any assumed benefit for the defendant.

Another way of viewing the fourth statutory assumption is that it places upon the defendant the burden of showing that others have an interest in any property in which he has an interest.

An interest refers to an interest in ownership, for example where property is owned jointly with another, or a legal interest, for example the interest of a mortgage lender in the property on which the mortgage is secured.

In many cases it will be straightforward to establish the interest of another in property in which the defendant has an interest, for example by a search of the Land Registry.

CHAPTER ELEVEN

THE DEFENDANT'S
SECTION 17 RESPONSE

The situation

On receipt of the prosecutor's s16(3) or 16(5) statement of information the defendant will have, for the first time, an indication of the benefit and available amount being asserted by the prosecution in the confiscation proceedings against him. The prosecutor's contentions may come as something of a shock to the defendant.

The defendant's s17 statement will be his detailed response to the prosecutor's assertions.

Responding to a poorly prepared s16(3) or 16(5) statement

The quality of prosecutors' s16(3) or 16(5) statements varies from case to case. Many are well prepared by financial investigators having a good understanding of confiscation law, the case proved against the defendant, and the defendant's financial circumstances.

Occasionally a s16(3) or 16(5) statement is issued which has been poorly prepared, lacking vital information or supporting documents. In such cases it may be appropriate, before submitting a s17 response, to request the prosecution to submit a revised or supplementary s16 statement so that the issues in the confiscation proceedings can be properly identified and addressed by the defendant.

In the majority of cases however it will be appropriate to prepare and submit a s17 response, albeit that the response may include a request for further documents and information in the form of a supplementary prosecutor's statement under s16(6).

The s17 response is essentially reactive, rather than proactive, although it may incorporate new information from the defendant and discussion of relevant points of law (including those dealt with in chapter 8 on the prosecutor's s16 statement).

For the purposes of illustration, and to assist practitioners, an example of a completed s17 response is produced at Appendix 3. This illustrative response is intended to be representative of a response to a typical s16 statement of information which the authors have encountered in a relatively simple factual situation.

The significance of accepting an assertion in the prosecutor's s16 statement

Where, in the s17 response, the defendant accepts an assertion in the prosecutor's s16 statement then the court may treat that as conclusive in relation to whether the defendant has a criminal lifestyle and the amount of his benefit in relation to the accepted assertion.[238]

However, the acceptance in a s17 response of a prosecutor's assertion that the defendant has benefited from conduct is not admissible in evidence in proceedings for any offence.[239]

The significance of failing to challenge an allegation in the prosecutor's s16 statement

Where, in the s17 response, the defendant fails to challenge an allegation in the prosecutor's s16 statement then the court may treat that as an acceptance of that allegation, except insofar as it relates to the amount of the defendant's benefit.[240]

It may therefore be appropriate to include within the s17 response a statement that the allegations in the s16 statement are denied except where expressly admitted.

---

[238] s17(2) & Crim PR 33.13 (7)(a)

[239] s17(6)

[240] s17(3) & Crim PR 33.13 (7)(b)

If the defendant, without reasonable excuse, fails to supply a s17 response the court may draw such inferences as it believes to be appropriate.[241]

The layout of the s17 response

As the s17 response is the defendant's detailed reply to the s16 statement it may be convenient, and it is appropriate, to deal with the content of the s16 statement paragraph by paragraph, admitting or denying each paragraph in turn[242] and where appropriate indicating what further documents, information, reasoning or explanations are sought from the prosecutor.

It may be, for example, that the prosecutor makes assertions without sufficient underpinning factual evidence, or without providing supporting legal argument where the legal position is open to doubt.

It may assist the parties and the court if the s17 response is split into separate documents as follows

- Concise pleadings as to the responses of the defendant to the matters upon which the prosecutor relies and any additional matters on which the defendant relies;

- Statements and any exhibits upon which the defendant relies; and

- If required, a skeleton argument.

This may assist in ensuring that evidence, submissions and the factual basis on which the case is put are readily discernible. This format was provisionally proposed by the Law Commission in its consultation paper on confiscation[243].

---

[241] Crim PR 33.13 (7)(c)

[242] Crim PR 33.13 (6)(a)

[243] Law Commission consultation paper 249, Confiscation of the proceeds of crime after conviction, September 2020

It may be appropriate for the s17 response to be prepared or reviewed by a lawyer with appropriate qualifications and experience.

Further information contained in the s17 response

The defendant will typically also be providing further detailed information within his s17 response (such as details of legitimate monies received) or may be providing supporting documents such as property valuations, mortgage statements or a forensic accountant's report.[244]

A forensic accountant's report is likely to be particularly useful where the prosecution assert that the defendant has a criminal lifestyle.

Alternatively, or additionally, the s17 response may indicate that further information and documents are to follow.

The defendant's available amount

With regard to his available amount the defendant should ensure that any interests held by others in property included within his available amount are either recognised in the prosecutor's statement or set out clearly in the s17 response.

Scott schedules

It may be appropriate to include schedules (sometimes referred to as 'Scott Schedules') in tabular form comparing the amounts contended by prosecution and defence for each of the elements of benefit and available amount, so that the differing respective positions can be readily appreciated.[245]

Proportionality

Where issues of proportionality – in the *Waya*[246] sense – arise, for example where any property obtained by the defendant has been made

---

[244] s17(1)(b) & Crim PR 33.13 (6)(b)

[245] Crim PR 33.13 (2)(c)(ii)

[246] *R v Waya [2012] UKSC 51*

good to the victim, these should be set out and, if possible, quantified in the s17 response, with a view to a possible reduction in the amount ordered to be paid.[247]

Benefit obtained jointly

Where benefit has been obtained jointly with one or more others (whether or not they are co-defendants) this should be made clear in the s17 response so that any confiscation order ultimately made may include an appropriate restriction on enforcement[248].

Serving the s17 response

Ordinarily the s17 response will be in the form of a witness statement signed by the defendant and incorporating a statement of truth[249]. The s17 response should be served on the prosecutor and the court.[250]

---

[247] s6(5)

[248] See *R v Ahmad [2014] UKSC 36*

[249] Crim PR 33.7 refers

[250] Crim PR 33.13 (2)(c)(i)

CHAPTER TWELVE

EXPERT WITNESSES

The term 'expert witness' has a technical meaning in court proceedings. The evidence of an expert witness may include his opinion, and in this respect expert evidence differs from the evidence of a witness of fact only. The expert witness may also, if it is needed, furnish the court with relevant information which is likely to be outside its experience and knowledge.[251]

In this connection an expert witness is doing more than simply drawing common-sense inferences from established facts or evidence.

However in offering the court his opinions an expert witness must help the court to achieve the overriding objective of dealing with cases justly by giving opinion evidence which is objective and unbiased, and within the expert's area or areas of expertise.[252]

An expert witness in criminal proceedings has express duties under Part 19 of the Criminal Procedure Rules and, if he is an expert instructed by the prosecution, he will be expected to have regard to the CPS Guidance for Experts' Evidence, Case Management and Unused Material which includes reference to his obligations under the Criminal Procedure and Investigations Act 1996 (sometimes summarised as 'retain, record and reveal').

There is therefore a distinction to be drawn between a skilled witness who simply draws together facts and information, presents them in a form in which they can readily be assimilated by the court and draws common-sense inferences from them; and an expert witness who also assists the court by giving opinion evidence within his areas of expertise and has additional obligations to the court.

---

[251] Criminal Practice Direction V Evidence 19A Expert Evidence at 19A.1

[252] Crim PR 19.2 (1)

A prosecutor's statement of information under s16 is not the statement of an expert witness. The author of the s16 statement should not express his own opinions in any area of expertise, nor should he seek to usurp the role of the legal advocate for the prosecution.

Similarly an expert witness, whether instructed by the prosecution or the defence, should not seek to make submissions on points of law (although it may be necessary for him to set out his understanding of the legal position so as to place into context the matters of fact and opinion he finds it appropriate to address in his expert evidence).

There is however no inherent bar on a police officer acting as an expert witness where he is in a position to give objective and unbiased evidence on a relevant topic within his area of expertise. In confiscation cases it is commonplace for a police officer to give expert evidence relating to the production, supply or value of controlled drugs, for example. When acting as an expert witness he will, of course, be subject to the same requirements of the Criminal Procedure Rules and, if applicable, the Criminal Procedure and Investigations Act 1996 as any other expert witness.

Statements of expert witnesses may typically be appended to, and referred to within, s16 statements of prosecutors and s17 responses of defendants.

It is for the court to determine what weight, if any, to give to the evidence of an expert witness. In practice however if the court is provided with expert opinion evidence which is unchallenged the court is likely to accept that evidence, unless it finds it to be inadmissible for some reason.

Funding for the defence to instruct an expert witness

Legal aid funding will normally be available to the legally aided defendant for the instruction of one or more expert witnesses relevant to a confiscation hearing. Generally the prior authority mechanism will be the most appropriate route for the defendant's solicitor to apply for this.

As a first step a fee estimate should be obtained from an appropriate expert.

Drug expert

Where a defendant's conviction is related to controlled drugs it will typically be the case that the asserted benefit of his particular criminal conduct includes the value of a quantity of drugs. The s16 statement should then be supported by an expert witness statement from a person with knowledge and experience concerning the production, supply or valuation of relevant drugs (typically a police officer from a specialist unit).

The defence will need to carefully review the use made by the author of the s16 statement of the evidence of the expert witness. For example, where the expert offers different figures for the value of the drugs depending upon the market in which they are to be sold, the defence will want to critically review the value on which the prosecution choose to rely in their computation of the defendant's benefit and the reason for that choice.

The defence may also wish to instruct an independent expert to review the opinions proffered by the expert instructed by the prosecution.

Property valuation expert

The valuations of land and buildings may be relevant to the defendant's benefit or available amount, or both.

Typically the author of the s16 statement will not seek a professional property valuation but may instead rely on open source material and websites.

Where the defendant believes this has resulted in an over-statement of his benefit or available amount (and particularly where the value is relevant to his benefit, or he does not intend to actually sell a property included in his available amount) it will be appropriate to obtain a professional property valuation from a valuer acting as an expert witness (for a fee).

Estate agents do offer free valuations to prospective vendors, but the risk here is that the agent may over-value the property to improve his prospects of being instructed on the sale of the property in due course.

The valuer should ideally visit the property to physically inspect it, internally and externally, and prepare a report based on an open market sale by a willing vendor to a willing buyer. The valuer may need to be provided with information about the tenure of the property.

Valuations of other assets

Depending upon the circumstances it may be appropriate to obtain professional valuations of works of art, antiques, crypto-currencies, etc. Similar considerations will apply.

Using a forensic accountant

A forensic accountant may prove useful to the defence in a number of ways.

Firstly the forensic accountant may undertake a detailed check and re-performance of work done by the author of the s16 statement to confirm that the transactions referred to in the s16 statement actually did occur as described. Some forensic accountants use software similar to that used by prosecutors to analyse bank transactions and search for duplications and patterns in those transactions.

Secondly the forensic accountant may critically review inferences drawn in the s16 statement relevant to the defendant's benefit and available amount.

Thirdly the forensic accountant will consider information available to him from the defendant and any witnesses on whom he proposes to rely, which is unavailable to the author of the s16 statement.

Where appropriate the forensic accountant can act as an expert witness in considering, for example, accounting records maintained by the defendant or the value of a business (or shares in a business) owned by the defendant.

More generally a forensic accountant can be valuable as a skilled witness drawing together facts and information, and presenting them in a form in which they can readily be assimilated by the court in relation to the defendant's contentions.

A forensic accountant can also be instructed by the prosecution, although in practice the prosecution are likely instead to rely upon an accredited financial investigator employed by the prosecuting authority where there are no specific issues requiring an external expert.

Meetings of experts

The court may sometimes request a 'meeting of experts' with a view to identifying and, as far as possible, resolving factual differences between the s16 statement and the report of the forensic accountant instructed by the defence.

Such meetings can be very useful, although 'meeting of experts' is something of a misnomer as the author of the s16 statement is not acting as an expert witness.

The forensic accountant is not however a representative of the defendant. He is acting in an independent capacity as an unbiased and objective witness with an over-riding duty to the court. He is therefore not in a position to agree any figures on behalf of the defendant, or to negotiate or mediate in any sense.

CHAPTER THIRTEEN

FURTHER SECTION 16
STATEMENTS & RESPONSES

The situation

Further to the prosecutor's first s16 statement he may submit one or more further statements of information under s16(6). These may be issued in response to a defendant's s17 statement, or in response to a court order or directions, or simply of the prosecutor's own volition.

The provisions of s16(6)

The prosecutor is entitled to issue a further s16 statement at any time, and must do so if ordered by the court.

The provisions relating to the acceptance of, or failure to challenge, an allegation in a s16 statement apply equally to allegations in a further statement under s16(6).

Amendments to asserted benefit and available amount

Whilst a further s16 statement need not assert any change to the figures of benefit and available amount asserted in a previous s16 statement, in practice there will normally be some amendment to one figure or both.

It is by no means unusual for a further s16 statement to assert higher figures for benefit and available amount than those previously put forward. The defendant may therefore feel that he has been disadvantaged by his s17 response and that the parties are moving further apart rather than working towards a compromise position acceptable to both.

In reality however, in most cases, a revised s16 statement will demonstrate that some agreement has been reached on some matters and the areas of dispute, and the nature of those disputes, will be clarified.

There are therefore advantages to both parties in exchanges of revised s16 and s17 statements prior to the day of the confiscation hearing.

Serving the further s17 response

Any further s17 response ordinarily will be in the form of a witness statement signed by the defendant and incorporating a statement of truth[253] and should be served on the prosecutor and the court.

---

[253] Crim PR 33.7 refers

CHAPTER FOURTEEN

THE DEFAULT SENTENCE

Where a confiscation order is made against a defendant it will identify a period of imprisonment, known as the default sentence, which the defendant is liable to serve in default of payment. This period is fixed by the Crown Court at the time the confiscation order is made and will be specified in the confiscation order.

If the defendant is obliged to serve all, or part, of the default sentence that will be consecutive to any sentence the defendant is obliged to serve in respect of the offences of which he has been convicted.

Fixing the length of the default sentence

Section 35 deals with the fixing of the default sentence when the court is making a confiscation order. Essentially section 35 employs the machinery of sections 129 and 132 of the Sentencing Code[254] relating to the enforcement of fines[255], to the enforcement of a confiscation order.

However, where a defendant serves a term of imprisonment in default that does not prevent the confiscation order from continuing to have effect so far as any other method of enforcement is concerned[256]. So, an outstanding amount can still be recovered as a debt after the default sentence has been served.

Section 35 (which was amended with effect from 1 June 2015) includes the following table of maximum default sentences which the court may fix, based upon the amount ordered to be paid under a confiscation order–

---

[254] Sentencing Act 2020

[255] Previously sections 139 and 140 Powers of Criminal Courts (Sentencing) Act 2000

[256] s38(5)

An amount of £10,000 or less	6 months
More than £10,000 but no more than £500,000	5 years
More than £500,000 but no more than £1 million	7 years
More than £1 million	14 years

These are maximum sentences. Although no minimum term is specified in the legislation, in practice the actual default sentence set by the court will typically be no less than the maximum of the band below and will be no more than the maximum for the band.

For example, where the amount to be paid is £600,000 the default sentence set by the court would typically be no less than 5 years (the maximum of the band below) and will be no more than 7 years (the maximum for the band).

It will normally be the case, in the absence of other important factors, that the default sentence for a higher amount required to be paid will be greater than that for a lower amount.

However, fixing the default sentence is not a mere mathematical exercise so that, for example, the default sentence for an amount to pay of £750,000 (which is mid-way between £500,000 and £1 million) will not automatically be fixed by the court at 6 years (which is mid-way between 5 years and 7 years).

The court is required to consider all the circumstances of the case when fixing the default term[257]. Where the court considers the defendant to be particularly uncooperative it may fix a default sentence at a higher figure to provide a greater encouragement for the defendant to cooperate.

---

[257] *R v Castillo [2011] EWCA Crim 3173*

Release at half time

The defendant will be entitled to be released unconditionally when he has served one-half of the default sentence[258], except that in connection with a default sentence for a sum which exceeds £10 million no release at half-time is required[259].

Early release for part payment

Where part, but not all, of the principal amount outstanding has been paid, the defendant's default sentence will be reduced pro-rata to the amount paid.

For example, Gerald has an amount to pay of £200,000 in respect of which the court fixed a default sentence of 30 months. Gerald has paid only £20,000 (one tenth of the amount due). His default sentence will be reduced pro-rata (by one tenth) to 27 months[260] (of which he will be obliged to serve no more than half).

In performing this calculation any interest which has been added to the amount due[261] is ignored[262].

Irrecoverable tainted gift

Where the defendant's available amount, and hence the amount ordered to be paid, includes the value of a tainted gift which is, in practice, not recoverable the court may take that into account and, exceptionally, fix a lower default sentence than might otherwise be appropriate[263].

---

[258] s258(2) Criminal Justice Act 2003

[259] s258(2B) Criminal Justice Act 2003

[260] In practice the calculation would be based on the number of days, not months

[261] s12 refers

[262] *R (Gibson) v Secretary of State for Justice [2018] UKSC 2*

[263] *R v Johnson [2016] EWCA Crim 10*

Very high value confiscation orders

Where the amount ordered to be paid exceeds £1 million the maximum term of the default sentence is 14 years. Prior to 1 June 2015 the maximum term was 10 years.

It may be useful to note that past case law has resulted in default terms of 10 years (the legal maximum at the time) for a sum of £12.6 million[264], 9 years for a sum of £3 million[265], and 8 years for a sum of £2.2 million[266].

Appeal against the default sentence

Whilst a defendant is able to appeal against the default sentence fixed in the Crown Court, the prosecution is not permitted to appeal solely against the default sentence where no appeal is being pursued against any other aspect of the confiscation order[267].

Default sentence where confiscation order varied

The position regarding the effect on the default sentence when a confiscation order is varied under s21, s22 or s23 (or under sections 29, 32 or 33) is not entirely straightforward. This is because s39[268] which deals with the default sentence in these circumstances only permits a variation in the default term where the variation in the amount ordered to be paid has the effect of varying the maximum default term set out in the table in s35 (reproduced above)[269].

---

[264] *Ahmad v R [2012] EWCA Crim 391*

[265] *R v Castillo [2011] EWCA Crim 3173*

[266] *R v Harvey [2013] EWCA Crim 1104*

[267] *R v Mills [2018] EWCA Crim 944*

[268] As amended with effect from 1 December 2020 by the Sentencing (Pre-consolidation Amendments) Act 2020 Schedule 2 Paragraph 121

[269] s39(1)(b)

Therefore, a change (whether an increase or reduction) in the amount ordered to be paid which does not move that amount from one band in that table to another, cannot result in a change to the default sentence.

For example, Henry was subject to a confiscation order made in 2016. His benefit was £400,000 and his available amount at that time was £25,000. Henry was ordered to pay £25,000 and the default sentence was set at 12 months. Henry paid the £25,000 in full and on time. In 2020 Henry received a legacy of £1 million. An application made under s22 resulted in the confiscation order being varied so that the amount to pay became £400,000 (of which £25,000 had already been paid). The court cannot vary the default term as the maximum default term set out in the table in s35 has not changed.

Where a confiscation order is varied so that the new amount required to be paid falls into a lower band, and the new maximum default sentence is less than the default sentence previously fixed by the court, the court must fix a reduced default sentence[270].

Where a confiscation order is varied so that the new amount required to be paid falls into a higher band than the previous amount required to be paid, the court may amend the default sentence[271].

Default sentence where interest added

Where interest added to the original amount required to be paid under a confiscation order causes the total amount payable to fall into a higher band in the table set out in s35, the court may amend the default sentence on an application by the prosecutor[272].

For example, Ingrid was subject to a confiscation order in 2018 under which she was required to pay £900,000 by 1 November 2018. The default sentence was fixed at 6 years 9 months in the confiscation order. Ingrid has paid nothing. With accrued interest the amount outstanding

---

[270] s39(2)

[271] s39(4)

[272] s39(5)

is now £1,044,000. As this amount falls into a higher band, the court may now amend Ingrid's default sentence on an application by the prosecutor.

CHAPTER FIFTEEN

THE CONFISCATION HEARING

If it has proved impossible to reach agreement, the issues between the parties will have to be determined in a contested confiscation hearing. The law to be applied in respect of confiscation is set out elsewhere in this book, so this short chapter is directed at the preparation that should be undertaken for the confiscation hearing and some practical matters that need to be considered.

Preparation

As set out earlier in this book, the burden is upon the defendant to establish the legitimacy of his assets. It is for the defendant to show on the balance of probabilities that the assumption in a criminal lifestyle case is incorrect or the assumption would cause a serious risk of injustice by the application of s.10(6): *R v Bagnall* [2012] EWCA Crim 677 at para.20.

If the presumption is to be rebutted, effective and careful planning and preparation is required well in advance of the hearing. At least 8 weeks before the hearing the following matters should be reviewed:

(1) Do the statements served on behalf of the defendant adequately deal with the matters raised by the prosecution? If they do not, then consideration should be given to serving a further addendum statement and/or ensuring that the relevant, additional, supporting evidence has been filed and served upon the court and the relevant parties.

(2) In the event that a report has been prepared by a forensic accountant or other expert, has there been further evidence served by the prosecution that the expert should be asked to consider? If so, this should be attended to as a matter of urgency. If the service

of an addendum report is unnecessary or unfeasible, solicitors should still ensure that counsel are aware of the expert's view regarding any issue that has been recently raised by the prosecution.

(3) Has a procedural and factual chronology been prepared? If not, a draft chronology should be prepared at this stage, which can be amended closer to the final hearing date.

(4) In the event that there have been applications for disclosure, the extent of the prosecution's compliance with those orders and requests should be reviewed. If there has been a lack of compliance, an application to enforce compliance should be considered at this stage.

At least 2 weeks before the hearing the following tasks should be undertaken:

(1) A conference should take place between solicitors, counsel and the defendant to ensure that the defendant is sufficiently appraised of the matters that are relevant and irrelevant for the purposes of the confiscation hearing.

(2) A paginated hearing bundle should be prepared and finalised between counsel, solicitors and client.

(3) The procedural and factual chronology should be finalised.

Ultimately, the defendant and his or her representatives should satisfy themselves that all relevant evidence that they wish to rely upon is before the court. If a defendant has failed to put relevant material before the court, that is very unlikely to give rise to a ground of appeal.

The preparation of a Scott Schedule prior to the hearing, briefly identifying the issues and the respective positions of the prosecution and defence, may prove to be of considerable practical value to the parties and the court. For the purposes of illustration, and to assist practitioners, an example of a Scott Schedule in a relatively simple factual situation is produced at Appendix 4.

The Procedure at the Hearing

The process is that the court will hear evidence from the witnesses for the Applicant and then the witnesses for the Respondent. It is important to remember that, as POCA hearings are quasi-civil, hearsay evidence can be admitted without the strict procedural requirements and legal gateways in criminal proceedings[273]. The court will then hear submissions from the parties' representatives and will provide a ruling that determines the appropriate benefit figure, available amount, amount required to be paid, time allowed for payment and default sentence.

In view of the possibility that the court may be requested to revisit the defendant's available amount or, less commonly, his benefit at a future date it is important that the court's detailed findings on these matters should be fully recorded following the conclusion of the hearing.

<u>Third Parties</u>

The involvement of third parties in confiscation proceedings can significantly complicate the issues that the court is asked to determine. If third parties are involved it is, therefore, crucial that their participation in the case is carefully case managed so that the court is in a position to determine the viability of resolving the issues within the context of a Crown Court hearing. It may be that if complex issues of trust and property law arise, consideration should be given to transferring the case to the Business and Property Courts or requesting that a High Court judge sit in the Crown Court to determine those matters[274]. It should also be borne in mind that the Crown Court can decline to make a determination under s.10A at the confiscation stage, leaving the matter to be dealt with at the enforcement stage with an enforcement receiver being appointed to deal with the issue.

---

[273] *R v Clipston* [2011] EWCA Crim 446 deals with admissibility of evidence in confiscation proceedings

[274] For an example of what can go wrong with the determination of civil matters in the Crown Court, see *R v Moore (Michael Robert)* [2021] EWCA Crim 956. See also *Moore at* [9] in relation to the approach to be taken when complex matters arise in confiscation proceedings

Other orders at the Conclusion of the Confiscation Hearing

The Sentence in Default

This is dealt with in Chapter 14.

Compensation

If the judge is minded to make a compensation order, then it is essential that counsel establish whether he intends to make an order for compensation to be paid from the confiscation order or whether he intends to make an order for compensation in addition to the confiscation order. If it is the former, then it must be recorded in the order with accuracy or the defendant may be required to pay significantly more than the judge intended[275].

The court has the power to make both a confiscation and a separate compensation order, but this will only be appropriate if the defendant has sufficient assets to satisfy both. The court should also consider the following before making two separate orders for compensation and confiscation:

(i) Would the order be disproportionate?

(ii) Has there been restitution to the victim? If so, a separate compensation order is likely to be inappropriate[276].

Payment of Prosecution Costs

In common with separate compensation orders, an order for payment of the prosecution's costs will only be appropriate if the Defendant has the additional assets to satisfy that order: *R v Ghadami* [1997] Crim LR 606.

---

[275] If an error in the wording of an order is not detected within the 56 day slip rule, then the Defendant will have to seek the intervention of the Court of Appeal Criminal Division. This could be embarrassing for all concerned.

[276] This will, however, involve an analysis of whether restitution has been paid in full and, if not, the explanation for any failure to make restitution before the hearing. See the guidance of the Court of Appeal in *R v Davenport* [2015] EWCA Crim 1731; [2016] 1 Cr App R (S) 41.

CHAPTER SIXTEEN

VARIATION TO CONFISCATION ORDERS

Reasons for variation

A confiscation order may be varied as a result of events occurring or information being received after the confiscation order has been made.

The most common variations are made to reduce the defendant's available amount under s23 where assets have been realised for less than expected, or to increase the amount required to be paid under s22 where a defendant has obtained an increased available amount since the confiscation order was made.

The court may discharge a confiscation order which has not been fully satisfied under s24, s25 or s25A where either the amount outstanding is modest, or the defendant has died, and it is not possible or not reasonable to recover anything further from his estate.

However, there are also circumstances in which the benefit figure found by the court can be revisited under s21.

Although strictly speaking not a variation, where the court has not made any confiscation order it may be obliged under s19 or s20 to reconsider whether to make a confiscation order.

Reduction in available amount under s23

When a confiscation order is made, the defendant's available amount will be assessed on the information available to the court at the time. This may include, for example, valuations of residential properties.

In the event the assets forming the defendant's available amount may subsequently be realised for less than the amounts anticipated when the order was made – particularly where assets need to be realised swiftly.

The assets forming the defendant's available amount and liabilities secured on those assets should be itemised on a schedule accompanying the confiscation order (form 5050A).

A s23 application will typically be made by (or on behalf of) the defendant, but may be made by a prosecutor or receiver[277]. There is no statutory time limit on the making of an application under s23 but, for obvious reasons, no s23 application will be made after the confiscation order has been fully satisfied.

It will be necessary in the s23 application to deal with every asset which was originally an element in the defendant's available amount when the confiscation order was made[278] (even if only to confirm that the asset has been realised and the proceeds used towards satisfying the order).

The essence of the s23 application is to identify the defendant's current available amount[279] and compare that to the amount remaining to be paid under the confiscation order. If the current available amount is less than the amount remaining to be paid, then the court has discretion to reduce the total amount required to be paid under the order.[280] If the application is successful, the court will normally reduce the amount required to be paid under the order so that the amount remaining to be paid equals the defendant's current available amount. However, the court has discretion to substitute for the amount required to be paid "such smaller amount as the court believes is just".

For example: Peter is subject to a confiscation order requiring him to pay £100,000. His benefit was a figure in excess of this. His available amount

---

[277] s23(1)(b)

[278] See *Gokal v Serious Fraud Office [2001] EWCA Civ 368* at paragraph [24], a case under Criminal Justice Act 1988 confiscation provisions

[279] s23(2)

[280] s23(3)

at the time the order was made was £100,000, comprising £20,000 in a bank account and £80,000 equity in a house. The £20,000 from the bank account has been paid, leaving £80,000 remaining to be paid. The house has now been sold, but after expenses of sale only £65,000 has been realised towards satisfying the £80,000 remaining to be paid. Peter has no other assets, so his current available amount is £65,000 which is less than the amount remaining to be paid. A s23 application is made successfully. The court reduces the amount required to be paid under the confiscation order to £85,000 (of which £20,000 has already been paid). This enables Peter to satisfy the order by paying the £65,000 realised from the sale of the house.

An incidental consequence of a s23 variation is that any outstanding accrued interest on the amounts payable under the order is expunged. This may be regarded as an added attraction to s23 orders from the defendant's point of view.

In practice the facts behind a s23 application may be uncontentious and this may lead to consent to a proposed s23 order. In these circumstances only, the court can make the s23 order without a hearing.[281]

The application for a s23 order must be in writing and may be supported by a witness statement.[282] It must be served on the court[283] and (if made by the defendant) on the prosecutor and any receiver.[284]

The application must identify any slavery and trafficking reparation order made by virtue of the confiscation order.[285]

For the purposes of illustration, and to assist practitioners, an example of an application for a variation under s23 in a relatively simple factual situation is produced at Appendix 5.

---

[281] CrimPR 33.17(5)(a)

[282] CrimPR 33.17(2)(a)

[283] CrimPR 33.17(3)

[284] CrimPR 33.17(4)

[285] CrimPR 33.17(2)(b)

Where an order by consent is applied for, a draft order and evidence of consent must accompany the application.[286]

The court's decision on a s23 application is not open to appeal to the Court of Appeal as it is not a 'sentence'.[287]

Where, as a result of a variation under s23 of the amount required to be paid, the maximum period of a default sentence applicable in relation to the order under the table set out in s35(2A) changes and is less than the term of imprisonment or detention fixed in the confiscation order then the court must fix a reduced term.[288]

Increase in available amount – application under s22

Where a confiscation order has been made requiring an amount to be paid which is based on the defendant's available amount at the time of the order, and his benefit was a larger figure, then the prosecutor (or a receiver) may subsequently apply to the court under s22 for the defendant's available amount to be considered afresh.[289] Where the court finds that the defendant's current available amount exceeds his available amount found at the time the order was made (after adjusting for changes in the value of money) the court has discretion to vary the amount required to be paid under the order.

An application under s22 might be made relatively soon after the confiscation order was made, for example where it comes to light that the defendant had assets which ought to have been included in his available amount when the order was made but were not, or might be made many years after the confiscation order, for example where the defendant has developed a successful legitimate business since the confiscation order was made. There is no statutory time limit on the making of a s22 application.

---

[286] CrimPR 33.17(2)(c)

[287] s50(1)(cb) Criminal Appeal Act 1968

[288] s39(1) & (2)

[289] s22(1)

The assets originally forming the defendant's available amount and liabilities secured on those assets should have been itemised on a schedule accompanying the confiscation order (form 5050A).

The essence of the s22 application is to identify the defendant's current available amount[290] and compare that to the available amount found at the time the order was made (or, if the order has previously been varied under s22, the available amount found at that time)[291] as adjusted for changes in the value of money.[292] If the current available amount is greater than that, then the court has discretion to vary the total amount required to be paid under the order.[293] The court then has discretion to substitute for the amount required to be paid "such amount as it believes is just but does not exceed the amount found as the defendant's benefit"[294] (after adjusting for changes in the value of money).[295]

For example: Simon was subject to a confiscation order in 2013 showing that he had a benefit of £200,000 and an available amount of £30,000. The order required him to pay £30,000. Simon paid the £30,000 in full and on time. In 2020 his father dies, leaving Simon a legacy of £100,000 which Simon places in a bank account in his name. On becoming aware of this, the prosecutor makes an application under s22. Simon also owns a car which he purchased in 2018 for £3,000 and is now valued at £2,000. There has been 10% inflation since 2013 (based on the CPIH index from the Office of National Statistics). So, adjusting the available amount of £30,000 which Simon had in 2013 for changes in the value of money produces a figure of £33,000 (£30,000 plus 10%). The court asks itself whether Simon's available amount today, of £102,000 (£100,000 plus £2,000), is greater than his 2013 available amount of £33,000. Of course, £102,000 is greater than £33,000. The court then has discretion to substitute for the amount required to be paid such amount as it believes is just (but not to exceed his benefit of £200,000 –

---

[290] s22(3)

[291] s22(8)

[292] s22(7)

[293] s22(4)

[294] s22(4)

[295] s22(7)

or £220,000 when the benefit figure is adjusted for changes in the value of money since 2013). In practice the prosecutor will invite the court to vary the amount required to be paid under the order to £132,000 (of which £30,000 has already been paid). If the court agrees, Simon will be required now to pay a further £102,000.

It is important that the court be taken to the detailed provisions of s22, following the necessary steps of calculating the defendant's current available amount, comparing that with his previously found available amount (adjusted for changes in the value of money), and checking whether the current available amount exceeds that figure. In the authors' experience prosecutors typically fail to draw the court's attention to the detailed provisions of s22 and fail to correctly consider whether the test inherent in the section has been satisfied.

Second example: Teresa was subject to a confiscation order in 2010 showing that she had a benefit of £300,000 and an available amount of £50,000. The order required her to pay £50,000. Teresa paid the £50,000, in full and on time. In 2020 Teresa wins £55,000 on the lottery which she places in a bank account in her name. On becoming aware of this, the prosecutor makes an application under s22. It transpires that Teresa has no other assets and has made no tainted gifts. There has been 20% inflation since 2010 (based on the CPIH index from the Office of National Statistics). So, adjusting the available amount of £50,000 which Teresa had in 2010 for changes in the value of money produces a figure of £60,000 (£50,000 plus 20%). The court asks itself whether Teresa's available amount today, of £55,000, is greater than her 2010 available amount, equivalent to £60,000. Of course, £55,000 is not greater than £60,000. It is arguable that, on a strict interpretation of the statute, the court has no opportunity on this occasion to vary Teresa's confiscation order under s22 and she should not be obliged to pay a further amount at this time.

This is because:

(a) s22(3) states that, "In a case where this section applies the court must make the new calculation, and in doing so must apply section 9 as if references to the time the confiscation order is made were to the time of the new calculation and as if references to the date of the confiscation order were to the date of the new calculation".

(b) s22(8) defines the relevant amount as the amount last found as the available amount

(c) s22(4) states that, "*If* (our emphasis) the amount found under the new calculation exceeds the relevant amount the court may vary the order by substituting for the amount required to be paid..."

In Teresa's case, the amount under the new calculation does not exceed the relevant amount.

On the other hand, the purpose of s22 is to provide the court with a discretion to increase the amount required to be paid to a figure "that it believes is just", provided that it does not exceed the benefit figure.

It may be that this is a matter that will ultimately have to be determined by the Court of Appeal Criminal Division.

In practice, it may be the case that a s22 application may be uncontentious and this may lead to consent to a proposed s22 order. In these circumstances only, the court can make the s22 order without a hearing.[296]

The application for a s22 order must be in writing and may be supported by a witness statement.[297] It must be served on the court[298] and (if made by the prosecutor) on the defendant and any receiver.[299]

The application must identify any slavery and trafficking reparation order made by virtue of the confiscation order.[300]

---

[296] CrimPR 33.16(5)(a)

[297] CrimPR 33.16(2)(a)

[298] CrimPR 33.16(3)

[299] CrimPR 33.16(4)

[300] CrimPR 33.16(2)(b)

Where an order by consent is applied for, a draft order and evidence of consent must accompany the application.[301]

The court's decision on a s22 application is open to appeal by the defendant to the Court of Appeal.[302] The Court of Appeal has heard appeals by the prosecution in relation to s22 variations however it appears that the issue as to whether the court should entertain such an appeal, which depends upon the scope of s31, has not been the subject of legal argument.

Where, as a result of a variation under s22 of the amount required to be paid, the effect of the variation is to vary the maximum period of a default sentence applicable in relation to the order under the table set out in s35(2A), then the court may amend the term of the default sentence.[303]

In practice in many cases the defendant will wish to argue that it would not be "just" for the confiscation order to be varied as the prosecution request. When considering what may be "just" the court should consider what is just to both the prosecution (in the public interest) and the defendant.

In the case of *Padda* the Court of Appeal noted, with regard to the court's discretion, "That discretion must of course be exercised in a way intended to "give effect to Parliament's intention as expressed in the language of the statute. The statutory language must be given a fair and purposive construction in order to give effect to its legislative policy": see *Waya*[304] paragraph 8. It is perfectly clear that the policy underlying POCA and its predecessors places a high priority on the recovery of the proceeds of crime".[305] The Court also noted, "In that context, it is entirely appropriate for a court to consider such matters as the amount outstanding, the additional amount which might now be available for a further payment, the length of time since the original confiscation order

---

[301] CrimPR 33.16(2)(c)

[302] s50(1)(cb) Criminal Appeal Act 1968

[303] s39(1), (3) & (4)

[304] *R v Waya [2012] UKSC 51*

[305] *Padda v R [2013] EWCA Crim 2330* at paragraph [42]

was made, the impact on the defendant of any further payment contemplated and indeed any other consideration which might properly be thought to affect the justice of the case".[306]

The focus of a s22 application will be on the defendant's current available amount. A s22 application is not an opportunity to challenge the existing confiscation order. However, it would not be "just" to order the defendant to pay an amount which, in the light of subsequent case law, would not now be regarded as benefit obtained by the defendant for confiscation purposes. Therefore it may be appropriate for the defendant to draw to the court's attention, when hearing a s22 application, matters which it now appears were not correctly addressed in fixing his benefit when the confiscation order was made. This will include, for example, a 'change of law' as a consequence of subsequent case law.[307]

Modest amount outstanding – discharge of a confiscation order under s24 or s25

Where a confiscation order has been made and not more than £50 remains to be paid under it, the designated officer for a magistrates' court may apply to the Crown Court to have the order discharged under s25. The Crown Court may then discharge the order.

Where a confiscation order has been made and less than £1,000 remains to be paid under it, the designated officer for a magistrates' court may apply to the Crown Court to have the order discharged under s24. In this event the Crown Court must calculate the defendant's current available amount. If it finds the current available amount is insufficient to satisfy the amount remaining to be paid and that this inadequacy is due wholly to a specified reason or a combination of specified reasons, it may discharge the order. A 'specified reason' may be where any of the realisable property consists of money in a currency other than sterling and that fluctuations in currency exchange rates have occurred. Other

---

[306] *Padda v R* at paragraph [45]

[307] See, for example, *R v Cole [2018] EWCA Crim 888* at paragraph [48]

'specified reasons' may be laid down by the Secretary of State for the purposes of s24.

Where an application for discharge is made by the designated officer for a magistrates' court the application must be in writing and must be served on the defendant, the prosecutor and any receiver.[308] If no notification is received with 7 days that a person would like to make representations on the application, the Crown Court may determine the application without a hearing.[309]

The Crown Court must serve notice of the discharge of the confiscation order on the magistrates' court, the defendant, the prosecutor and any receiver.[310]

Defendant deceased – discharge of a confiscation order under s25A

Where a confiscation order has been made and the defendant has died whilst a sum remains to be paid under the order, the designated officer for a magistrates' court may apply to the Crown Court to have the order discharged under s25A. If it appears to the Crown Court that either it is not possible to recover anything from the estate of the deceased to satisfy the order, or it would not be reasonable to make any further attempt to recover anything from the estate of the deceased, then the Crown Court may discharge the order.

Revisiting the benefit figure under s21

Where the court has made a confiscation order and there is evidence which was not available to the prosecutor when the court calculated (or last calculated) the defendant's benefit, and the prosecutor now believes that the defendant's benefit is greater than the figure of benefit found (or last found)[311] by the court (after taking into account changes in the value

---

[308] CrimPR 33.18(3)

[309] CrimPR 33.18(4)

[310] CrimPR 33.18(5)

[311] s21(13)

of money)[312], the prosecutor may apply to the Crown Court to reconsider the defendant's benefit under s21.

The prosecutor's application must be made no later than six years[313] after the date of the defendant's conviction of 'the offence concerned'.[314] Where there is more than one date of conviction the six-year period commences on the day of the latest conviction.[315]

If, after hearing the evidence, the court considers it appropriate to proceed under s21 it must make a new calculation of the defendant's benefit.[316] For that purpose the court places itself back in time to the date on which it decided the defendant's benefit (effectively the day on which the confiscation order was made) but reconsiders the defendant's benefit with the assistance of the evidence which was not available to the prosecutor at that time, except that it may take account of property obtained by the defendant after that time if it was obtained as a result of or in connection with conduct which occurred before that time.[317]

This process involves the court using the machinery of sections 6 to 10 and sections 16 to 18 with modifications, to recalculate the defendant's benefit and, in effect, re-make the confiscation order.

For the purposes of this recalculation of the defendant's benefit the statutory assumptions of s10 do not apply to any period after the day on which the confiscation order was made.[318]

If the court finds that the defendant's benefit is greater than the figure of benefit found (or last found)[319] by the court (after taking into account

---

[312] s21(11)

[313] s21(1)(d)

[314] See s6(2) & (9)

[315] s21(14) & s19(10)

[316] s21(1)(e) & (2)

[317] s21(4)(c)

[318] s21(6)

[319] s21(13)

changes in the value of money)[320], the court must make a new calculation of the defendant's current 'recoverable amount' (based on the new figure of benefit and the defendant's current available amount).[321] If the current 'recoverable amount' exceeds the amount required to be paid under the confiscation order (after taking account of changes in the value of money)[322], the court has discretion to vary the amount required to be paid to such amount as it believes is just.[323]

If the current 'recoverable amount' does not exceed the amount required to be paid under the confiscation order (after taking account of changes in the value of money), the court has no opportunity to vary the amount required to be paid under the confiscation order. However, in this event, the court's finding of an increased benefit figure should be recorded because it will be relevant to any subsequent application for a variation of the confiscation order under s22.[324]

In reaching its decision on the amount it believes is just the court must have regard to certain specified matters[325] and must not have regard to others.[326]

For example: Jane was convicted of a 'criminal lifestyle' offence and was subject to a confiscation order in 2017 showing that she had a benefit of £50,000. At that time Jane was believed to have an available amount of £70,000, which was a balance in a bank account in her sole name. The order required her to pay £50,000, which was the 'recoverable amount'. Jane paid the £50,000 in full and on time (leaving her with £20,000 in the bank). In 2020 the prosecutor discovered that when the confiscation order was made in 2017 Jane was also the owner of a residential property, subject to a mortgage. The equity in the property when the confiscation order was made was £40,000. Jane still owns the property. The equity in

---

[320] s21(11)

[321] s21(7)(a) & (8)

[322] s21(11)

[323] s21(7)(b)

[324] See s22(9)

[325] s21(9)

[326] s21(10)

the property today is £45,000. Jane still has £20,000 in the bank. On becoming aware of this, the prosecutor makes an application under s21. There has been 5% inflation since 2017 (based on the CPIH index from the Office of National Statistics). The prosecutor seeks to have the equity in the property of £40,000 in 2017 added to the benefit of £50,000 under the s10 assumption of property held after the date of conviction. He asks the court to vary the order so that Jane's benefit figure will be £90,000 (£50,000 plus £40,000). This exceeds the original benefit figure which, after adjusting for changes in the value of money, is £52,500 (£50,000 plus 5%). The court agrees that Jane's benefit figure in the confiscation order should be £90,000. The court calculates Jane's current available amount as £65,000 (her £20,000 bank balance and £45,000 equity in the property). The court finds Jane's current 'recoverable amount' is £65,000 (as her available amount of £65,000 is less than her benefit of £90,000). As her current 'recoverable amount' of £65,000 exceeds her previous 'recoverable amount' which, after adjusting for changes in the value of money, is £52,500 (£50,000 plus 5%) the court has discretion to vary the amount required to be paid under Jane's confiscation order. In practice the prosecutor will invite the court to vary the amount required to be paid under the order to £90,000 (of which £50,000 has already been paid). If the court agrees, Jane will be required now to pay a further £40,000.

Occasionally it may be the case that a s21 application may be uncontentious and this may lead to consent to a proposed s21 order. In these circumstances only, the court can make the s21 order without a hearing.[327]

Sections 16 to 18 apply (with appropriate modifications) to an application for a s21 order.[328] The information provided by the prosecutor must include details of the confiscation order which is sought to be varied.[329]

---

[327] CrimPR 33.15(4)(a)

[328] s26

[329] CrimPR 33.15(2)(a)

Where an order by consent is applied for, a draft order and evidence of consent must accompany the application.[330]

The court's decision on a s21 application is open to appeal by the defendant or the prosecutor to the Court of Appeal in the same way as any other confiscation order made under s6.[331]

Where, as a result of a variation under s21 of the amount required to be paid, the effect of the variation is to vary the maximum period of a default sentence applicable in relation to the order under the table set out in s35(2A), then the court may amend the term of the default sentence.[332]

In practice in many cases the defendant will wish to argue that it would not be "just" for the confiscation order to be varied as the prosecution request. When considering what may be "just" the court should consider what is just to both the prosecution (in the public interest) and the defendant.

Reconsideration under s19 or s20 of whether a confiscation order should be made

Where the court has not made any confiscation order and there is evidence which was not available to the prosecutor on the 'relevant date'[333], the prosecutor may apply to the Crown Court under s19 or s20 to consider, or reconsider, the making of a confiscation order.

The prosecutor's application must be made no later than six years[334] after the date of the defendant's conviction of 'the offence concerned'.[335]

---

[330] CrimPR 33.15(2)(b)

[331] s50(1)(cb) Criminal Appeal Act 1968

[332] s39(1), (3) & (4)

[333] Note the 'relevant date' referred to in relation to the variation of a confiscation order should not be confused with the 'relevant day' referred to elsewhere in relation to the statutory assumptions and tainted gifts

[334] s19(1)(c) & s20(4)(b)

[335] See s6(2) & (9)

Where there is more than one date of conviction the six-year period commences on the day of the latest conviction.[336]

Where initially the Crown Court has not been asked to consider making a confiscation order, and has not considered making one of its own volition, or the court made a decision not to proceed under s6, then the prosecutor's application will be under s19. The 'relevant date' on which information was not available to the prosecutor will be the date of the defendant's conviction (or latest date of conviction) or, if later, the date on which the court made a decision not to proceed under s6.[337]

If, after considering the evidence now available, the court believes it is appropriate to proceed under s6 then it must do so.[338]

For that purpose the court places itself back in time to the 'relevant date' but reconsiders the defendant's benefit with the assistance of the evidence which was not available to the prosecutor at that time, except that it may take account of property obtained by the defendant on or after that time if it was obtained as a result of or in connection with conduct which occurred before that time.[339]

This process involves the court using the machinery of sections 6 to 10 and sections 16 to 18[340] with modifications, to make a confiscation order.

For the purposes of the calculation of the defendant's benefit the statutory assumptions of s10 do not apply to any period on or after the 'relevant date'.[341]

The defendant's current available amount is calculated by the court under s9.

---

[336] s19(10) & s20(13)

[337] s19(9)

[338] s19(1)(d) & (2), s20(4)(c) & (5)

[339] s19(4)(c), s20(8)(c)

[340] s26

[341] s19(5)

The court has discretion to fix the amount required to be paid to such amount as it believes is just, but does not exceed the 'recoverable amount' found under s7.[342]

In reaching its decision on the amount it believes is just the court must have regard to certain specified matters.[343]

A confiscation order made under this procedure will be subject to appeal by the defendant or the prosecutor to the Court of Appeal in the same way as any other confiscation order made under s6.

Where initially the Crown Court has considered making a confiscation order but had concluded that the defendant had obtained no benefit and had accordingly made no confiscation order, then the prosecutor's application will be under s20. The 'relevant date' on which information was not available to the prosecutor will be the date on which the court concluded that the defendant had obtained no benefit for confiscation purposes.[344]

If, after considering the evidence now available, the court concludes that it would have decided that the defendant did obtain a benefit for confiscation purposes, then it must make a fresh decision under s6(4)(b) or (c) and may make a confiscation order.[345]

For that purpose the court places itself back in time to the relevant date but reconsiders the defendant's benefit with the assistance of the evidence which was not available to the prosecutor at that time, except that it may take account of property obtained by the defendant on or after that time if it was obtained as a result of or in connection with conduct which occurred before that time.[346]

---

[342] s19(6)

[343] s19(7) & (8)

[344] s20(4)(a)

[345] s20(4)(c) & (5)

[346] s20(8)(c)

This process involves the court using the machinery of sections 6 to 10 and sections 16 to 18[347] with modifications, to make a confiscation order.

For the purposes of the calculation of the defendant's benefit the statutory assumptions of s10 do not apply to any period on or after the relevant date.[348]

The defendant's current available amount is calculated by the court under s9.

The court has discretion to fix the amount required to be paid to such amount as it believes is just, but does not exceed the 'recoverable amount' found under s7.[349]

In reaching its decision on the amount it believes is just the court must have regard to certain specified matters.[350]

A confiscation order made under this procedure will be subject to appeal by the defendant or the prosecutor to the Court of Appeal in the same way as any other confiscation order made under s6.

---

[347] s26

[348] s20(9)

[349] s20(10)

[350] s20(11) & (12)

CHAPTER SEVENTEEN

ABSENT DEFENDANT

A confiscation order may be made in circumstances in which the defendant is not present at the confiscation hearing. Some of these circumstances are explicitly considered in the legislation, whilst others follow from wider principles.

Under common law principles the court can proceed to make a confiscation order where the defendant has voluntarily absented himself from court.

However, no confiscation order can be made where the defendant has been involuntarily deported[351], or has died, before the confiscation order is made. In these circumstances consideration may be given instead to proceedings under Part 5, POCA 2002 (civil recovery).

Defendant absconds before trial, confiscation under s28

Where a defendant has absconded before trial and has not been acquitted a confiscation order may be made, even in the absence of a conviction. This is the only circumstance in which a conviction is not required prior to the making of a confiscation order.

Section 28 deals with the defendant who absconds before trial. Although the section is headed "Defendant neither acquitted nor convicted" in practice this section is also used in the case of a defendant who absconded before his trial and has since been convicted in his absence.[352]

---

[351] *Gavin and Tasie [2010] EWCA Crim 2727*

[352] *R v Okedare [2014] EWCA Crim 1173*

Under the section it is incumbent upon the prosecutor to make application to the court, which will then decide if it believes it is appropriate to proceed.[353]

The section requires that proceedings for an offence, or offences have started[354] but have not concluded, and that the defendant has absconded at least three months previously.[355] It should be noted that confiscation purposes proceedings are not concluded on the defendant's conviction but are concluded, for example, when a confiscation order is satisfied.[356]

The section employs the confiscation machinery of s6 with modifications. In particular, the requirements for the defendant to provide information are disapplied.[357]

Importantly the statutory assumptions of s10 cannot be employed where the defendant has absconded.[358] The defendant in these circumstances would be unable to address and rebut the statutory assumptions.

The disapplication of the requirements for the defendant to provide information, and of the statutory assumptions, may result in a benefit figure which is substantially less than would have been the case if the defendant had not absconded.

Under the s28 provisions, any person whom the court believes is likely to be affected by the confiscation order is entitled to appear and be represented at the confiscation hearing.[359]

---

[353] s28(3)

[354] As to which see s85(1)

[355] s28(2)

[356] s85

[357] s28(5)(d)

[358] s28(5)(d)

[359] s28(5)(a)

The prosecutor who relies on s28 is required to have taken reasonable steps to contact the defendant.[360]

Where a confiscation order has been made under s28 and subsequently the defendant is convicted of the offence (or any of the offences) concerned then section 6 does not apply to those convictions[361], with the result that the defendant is not subject to a second set of confiscation proceedings in relation to the same offence.

If the absconder returns and is convicted and he believes that the amount required to be paid under the confiscation order which has been made under s28 is too large (based upon the circumstances prevailing when the confiscation order was made) he can, within 28 days[362] of the date of his conviction, apply to the court[363] to have the confiscation order varied to such amount as the court believes is just.[364]

The defendant's application to the court must be in writing and supported by a witness statement which must give details of (a) the confiscation order, (b) any slavery and trafficking reparation order made by virtue of the confiscation order, (c) the circumstances in which the defendant ceased to be an absconder, (d) the defendant's conviction of the offence or offences concerned, and (e) the reason why the defendant believes the amount required to be paid under the confiscation order was too large.[365] The application must be served on the court and the prosecution.[366]

If the absconder returns the prosecutor may apply to the court under s21 to have his benefit reconsidered.[367] In these circumstances the normal confiscation provisions, including requirements for the defendant to

---

[360] s28(5)(b)

[361] s28(7)

[362] s29(3)

[363] s29(1)

[364] s29(2)

[365] Crim PR 33.19(2)

[366] Crim PR 33.19(3) & (4)

[367] s28(6)

supply information[368] and the statutory assumptions[369] relating to benefit, can apply with modifications. The provisions of s21 are dealt with in chapter 16.

If the absconder returns, is tried, and acquitted on all counts (or if the prosecution offer no evidence[370]), the court must discharge the confiscation order made under s28.[371]

In other cases the returned absconder may apply to the Crown Court to discharge the order where it appears that the prosecutor does not intend to proceed with the prosecution or there has been undue delay in continuing the proceedings.[372]

The application must be in writing and supported by a witness statement which must give details of (a) the confiscation order, (b) the date on which the defendant ceased to be an absconder, (c) the acquittal of the defendant if he has been acquitted of the offence concerned, and (d) if the defendant has not been acquitted of the offence concerned (i) the date on which the defendant ceased to be an absconder, (ii) the date on which the proceedings taken against the defendant were instituted and a summary of steps taken in the proceedings since then, and (iii) any indication that the prosecutor does not intend to proceed against the defendant.[373] The application must be served on the court and the prosecution.[374]

---

[368] See s26

[369] s21(6)

[370] See s17 Criminal Justice Act 1967

[371] s30(1) & (2)

[372] s30(3) & (4)

[373] Crim PR 33.20(2)

[374] Crim PR 33.20(3) & (4)

If the court discharges the confiscation order the court officer must serve notice on any other court responsible for enforcing the order[375] and the court may make appropriate consequential or incidental orders.[376]

If the court varies or discharges a confiscation order made under s28, a person who held realisable property and has suffered loss as a result of the making of the order may apply for compensation under s73. The application must be in writing and supported by a witness statement which must give details of (a) the confiscation order, (b) the variation or discharge of the confiscation order, (c) the realisable property to which the application relates, and (d) the loss suffered by the applicant as a result of the confiscation order.[377] The application must be served on the court and the prosecution.[378]

Defendant absconds after conviction, confiscation under s27

Where a defendant has absconded after being convicted, but before a confiscation order has been made, a confiscation order may be made under s27.

Under the section it is incumbent upon the prosecutor to make application to the court, which will then decide if it believes it is appropriate to proceed.[379]

The section employs the confiscation machinery of s6 with modifications. In particular, the requirements for the defendant to provide information are disapplied.[380]

---

[375] Crim PR 33.20(5)

[376] s30(5)

[377] Crim PR 33.23(2)

[378] Crim PR 33.23(3) & (4)

[379] s27(3)

[380] s27(5)(d)

Importantly the statutory assumptions of s10 cannot be employed where the defendant has absconded.[381] The defendant in these circumstances would be unable to address and rebut the statutory assumptions.

The disapplication of the requirements for the defendant to provide information, and of the statutory assumptions, may result in a benefit figure which is substantially less than would have been the case if the defendant had not absconded.

Under the s27 provisions, any person whom the court believes is likely to be affected by the confiscation order is entitled to appear and be represented at the confiscation hearing.[382]

The prosecutor who relies on s27 is required to have taken reasonable steps to contact the defendant.[383]

If the absconder returns the prosecutor may apply to the court under sections 19, 20 or 21 to have confiscation proceedings in his case reconsidered.[384] In these circumstances the normal confiscation provisions, including requirements for the defendant to supply information[385] and the statutory assumptions[386] relating to benefit, can apply with modifications. The provisions of these sections are dealt with in chapter 16.

---

[381] s27(5)(d)

[382] s27(5)(a)

[383] s27(5)(b)

[384] s27(5)(e), (6) & (7)

[385] See s26

[386] See ss 19(5), 20(9) & 21(6)

CHAPTER EIGHTEEN

APPEALS

The 56-day Slip Rule

The Crown Court has the power to alter a sentence within 56 days beginning on the day on which the sentence was imposed. This power arises from the "slip rule" under s.385(2) of the Sentencing Act 2020. As confiscation is part of the sentencing process, the Crown Court has the power to vary a confiscation order within the same period as that provided for under s.385(2).

In the event that an error in a confiscation order is not corrected within 56 days, the only available remedy will be an appeal to the Court of Appeal Criminal Division.

Appeals to the Court of Appeal Criminal Division in Respect of a Confiscation Order

A Defendant's right to appeal a confiscation order arises from the Criminal Appeal Act 1968. Section 50(1) of the Criminal Appeal Act 1968 defines 'sentence' as including a confiscation order.

The Court of Appeal Criminal Division's Guide to Commencing Proceedings was released in July 2021. It contains the most up to date guidance in respect of proceedings before the Court of Appeal Criminal Division and is freely and easily available online[387]. It should be consulted before commencing a confiscation appeal, or indeed any appeal, as it helpfully summarises the processes and requirements of the Court.

---

[387] https://www.judiciary.uk/wp-content/uploads/2021/07/The-Court-of-Appeal-Division-Guide-to-Commencing-Proceedings.pdf

The Process of Appealing a confiscation order

An appeal is commenced by filing Form NG and signed grounds of appeal upon the Registrar of Criminal Appeals. A separate form NG should be filed for each substantive appeal. There is a specific Form NG for confiscation appeals[388]. Electronic filing is preferred and, if possible, the form NG and grounds of appeal should be sent to application@criminalappealoffice.justice.gov.uk, which will result in an acknowledgement being sent to the Applicant's representatives.

If serving by post the relevant address is the Criminal Appeal Office, Royal Courts of Justice, Strand, London, WC2A 2LL.

Where fresh legal representatives are instructed, it is now a strict requirement that the fresh representatives will make enquiries of those who were previously instructed. The obligations are those that are set out in *R v McCook* [2014] EWCA Crim 734. Those obligations also apply to appeals that relate to sentence: *R v Roberts & Others* [2016] EWCA Crim 71.

It is also important to note that a prosecutor should be given the opportunity to be present at a Defendant's appeal in respect of a confiscation order and to make submissions. The Court of Appeal consider that this is appropriate given the complexity that is often involved in appeals arising from confiscation orders[389].

Time Limits

Notice and grounds of appeal should be lodge within 28 days from the date of the confiscation order having been made.

If an application is made out of time, then an application for an extension of time should be made at the same time as the service of Form NG and the grounds of appeal. In *R v Jogee* [2016] UKSC 8 at [100] the Supreme

---

[388] https://www.gov.uk/government/publications/criminal-appeal-office-form-ng-confiscation-order

[389] See *R v Court (Ian Robert)* [2021] EWCA Crim 242

Court confirmed that the test in considering an application for leave to appeal out of time is whether any substantial injustice has been done.

The Court's Powers

The Court of Appeal has the power to substitute a new confiscation order in place of the order made by the Crown Court: *R v Hirani* [2008] EWCA Crim 1463.

If the confiscation order is quashed, then the Court may order that the Crown Court should hear the confiscation proceedings afresh and must give relevant directions to ensure that any subsequent order is not more severe than that which was originally passed[390].

Prosecutor's Right of Appeal

Section 31(1) of POCA, provides a prosecutor with a right of appeal in respect of a confiscation order made by the Crown Court and s.31(2) POCA provides a right of appeal where the Crown Court has declined to make a confiscation order.

Where the Crown Court has made a confiscation order then under s31(1) the Court of Appeal can confirm, vary or quash the order – but apparently cannot remit the order to the Crown Court for the purpose of finding additional facts[391]. In contrast where the Crown Court has not made a confiscation order the prosecution can appeal under s31(2) and the Court of Appeal can, amongst other things, remit the matter to the Crown Court for it to proceed afresh under s6. For this reason it is preferable for the Crown Court to make findings of fact on matters – even those which will become relevant only on a successful appeal – and so decisions simply on preliminary issues of law are to be discouraged.

---

[390] s.11(3) and (3A) of the Criminal Appeals Act 1968

[391] *London Borough of Barnet v Kamyab* [2021] EWCA Crim 543, although it is not clear whether s11(3A) Criminal Appeal Act 1968 was drawn to the court's attention

A prosecutor has no right of appeal against the default sentence alone in the absence of any appeal against another component of the confiscation order[392].

There are express limitations under s31(3) on the prosecutor's right of appeal in relation to decisions made under s.10A[393], s.19, s.20, s.27 or s.28.

Appeals by Third Parties

Third parties who have sought to determine their beneficial interest in property, pursuant to s.10A POCA, have a right of appeal under s.32(4) and (5) POCA, subject to the requirements of s.31(6) and s.31(7) POCA. Those sections require that either a party was not given a reasonable opportunity to be heard or that the Crown Court's determination would lead to substantial injustice against the Applicant.

The Court's Power in respect of s.10A Appeals

Pursuant to s.32(2A) POCA, the Court of Appeal has the power to either confirm the determination or make any order as it believes is appropriate.

Appeals relating to variations of a confiscation order

A defendant may appeal against a decision to vary an existing confiscation order under s22, as this variation is a 'sentence'[394]. The Court of Appeal has certainly heard a prosecutor's appeal on a s22 variation application[395], but it appears that whether the court had jurisdiction to hear that appeal may not have been argued. It might be suggested that under s22 a Crown Court does not 'make' a confiscation order (it 'varies' or declines to vary

---

[392] *R v Mills* [2018] EWCA Crim 944

[393] save in circumstances where the prosecutor submits that they were not given a reasonable opportunity to the heard or there would be substantial injustice – s.31(6) and s.31(7)

[394] s50(1) Criminal Appeal Act 1968

[395] *R v Mundy* [2018] EWCA Crim 105

an existing order) and therefore this falls outside the scope of s31(1) and (2).

No appeal is possible against a decision to vary (or decline to vary) a confiscation order under s23, as this is not a 'sentence'.

Appeals to the Supreme Court in Respect of a Confiscation Order

Section 33(1) POCA, provides a defendant or prosecutor with a right of appeal against the Court of Appeal's determinations in respect of a confiscation appeal. Those rights are, however, restrained by the requirement that an appeal lies only with the leave of the Court of Appeal or the Supreme Court and leave is likely to be granted rarely. The strict requirement for the granting of leave to the Supreme Court is that the matter raised is a point of law of general public importance and one that should be heard by the Supreme Court.

Time Limits

An application to the Court of Appeal for leave must be made within 28 days of the decision of the Court of Appeal. An application for leave to the Supreme Court must be made within 28 days of the Court of Appeal's refusal of an application for leave to appeal to the Supreme Court.

In respect of an appeal, by a defendant or prosecutor, against a prosecutor's appeal the time limits are shorter. An application to the Court of Appeal for leave must be made within 14 days of the decision of the Court of Appeal or, if later, the date of its judgment. An application for leave to the Supreme Court must be made within 14 days of the Court of Appeal's refusal of an application for leave to appeal to the Supreme Court.

The Court's Powers

The Supreme Court can vary, quash or confirm a confiscation order and may direct the Crown Court to proceed afresh.

Appeals to the Court of Appeal in Respect of a Restraint Order

Prosecutor's Appeals

Section 43(1) POCA provides a mechanism for an appeal to the Court of Appeal Criminal Division against a Crown Court's decision not to make a Restraint Order.

Appeal by a Defendant or Person affected by a Restraint Order

A defendant or person affected by a restraint order is required, in the first instance, to challenge the imposition of a restraint order, or to seek its variation or discharge, by applying to the Crown Court. At the conclusion of that process a defendant or person affected by a restraint order can then apply to the Court of Appeal Criminal Division for leave to appeal against the Crown Court's decision[396].

The Process of Appealing a Restraint Order

The appeal is commenced by serving Form POCA 3[397] on the Crown Court within 28 days of the decision being appealed. Form POCA 3 must then be served on any respondent and any person who holds realisable property to which the appeal relates, or is affected by the appeal, not later than seven days after the form is lodged at the Crown Court.

A Respondent's notice Form POCA 4[398] is to be served on the Registrar of Criminal Appeals not later than 14 days after the respondent is notified that the appellant has leave to appeal or notified that the application for leave and the appeal are to be heard together. Form POCA 4 is then to be served on the appellant and any other respondent as soon as is practicable and not later than seven days after it was served on the Registrar.

---

[396] s.43(2)

[397] https://www.gov.uk/government/publications/notice-and-grounds-of-application-for-leave-to-appeal-and-appeal-about-compliance-restraint-or-receivership-decision

[398] https://www.gov.uk/government/publications/respondents-notice-and-grounds-of-opposition-to-appeal-about-compliance-restraint-or-receivership-decision

CHAPTER NINETEEN

ACTIVATING THE DEFAULT SENTENCE

The activation of the default sentence is a matter for the Magistrates' Court at an enforcement hearing and is not a matter for the Crown Court.

Magistrates' Court's Powers

Section 76(2) of the Magistrates' Court Act 1980 ("**MCA**") provides the Magistrates' Court with power to issue a warrant of commitment, to activate the default term of imprisonment imposed by the Crown Court, in the event of non-payment of a confiscation order.

If a defendant fails to attend at a Magistrates' Court where an enforcement hearing has been convened, the Court may issue a warrant for his arrest pursuant to s.83 MCA: *R (Carlos Lawson) v City of Westminster Magistrates' Court* [2013] EWHC 2434 (Admin) and *R (Hickman) v Governor of HMP Wayland* [2016] EWHC 719 (Admin).

The default term may not be activated except in very limited circumstances. Those circumstances are set out at s.82(5A) – (5F) MCA:

> (5A) A Magistrates' Court may not issue a warrant of commitment under subsection (5) above at a hearing at which the offender is not present unless the designated officer for the court has first served on the offender a notice in writing stating that the court intends to hold a hearing to consider whether to issue such a warrant and giving the reason why the court so intends.

> (5B) Where after the occasion of an offender's conviction by a Magistrates' Court the court holds a hearing for the purpose of considering whether to issue a warrant of commitment for default in paying a sum adjudged to be paid by the

conviction, it shall consider such information about the offender's means as is available to it unless it has previously—

    (a)   inquired into the offender's means; and

    (b)   postponed the issue of the warrant of commitment under section 77(2) above.

(5C) A notice under subsection (5A) above—

    (a)   shall state the time and place appointed for the hearing; and

    (b)   shall inform the offender that, if he considers that there are grounds why the warrant should not be issued, he may make representations to the court in person or in writing, but the court may exercise its powers in relation to the issue of a warrant whether or not he makes representations.

(5D) Except as mentioned in subsection (5E) below, the time stated in a notice under subsection (5A) above shall not be earlier than 21 days after the issue of the notice.

(5E) Where a Magistrates' Court exercises in relation to an offender the power conferred by section 77(2) above and at the same hearing issues a notice under subsection (5A) above in relation to him, the time stated in the notice may be a time on any day following the end of the period for which the issue of the warrant of commitment has been postponed.

(5F) A notice under subsection (5A) above to be served on any person shall be deemed to be served on that person if it is sent by registered post or the recorded delivery service addressed to him at his last known address, notwithstanding that the notice is returned as undelivered or is for any other reason not received by that person.

General Principles

The Magistrates' Court must consider all other methods short of committal to prison for non-payment before doing so: *R v Harrow Justices ex parte DPP* [1991] 83 Cr. App. R. 388 QBD.

The Magistrates' Court should not impose a default sentence where real property is being actively marketed: *Barnett v DPP* [2009] EWHC 2004 (Admin).

The Magistrates' Court should not issue a warrant of commitment until the court has enquired into the means of the subject of the confiscation order and satisfied itself that the default is attributable to wilful refusal or culpable neglect by the subject of the confiscation order: *R (on the application Sanghera) v Birmingham Magistrates' Court* [2017] EWHC 3323 (Admin)

The Magistrates' Court should not issue a warrant of commitment where a defendant has not been given a reasonable opportunity to obtain adequate legal representation: *R (on the application of Agogo) v North Somerset Magistrates' Court* [2011] EWHC 518 (Admin)

The Magistrates' Court is only concerned with the enforcement of the order and if a defendant claims that his assets are insufficient to meet the confiscation order, he can invite the Crown Court to adjust the confiscation order pursuant to s.23 POCA. It will often be appropriate for the Magistrates' Court to adjourn the enforcement hearing pending the outcome of that application – lest a defendant be committed to a term of imprisonment in respect of a sum of money that he simply cannot pay.

CHAPTER TWENTY

A SECOND OR SUBSEQUENT CONFISCATION ORDER

Additional issues can arise where the defendant facing confiscation proceedings has previously been the subject of an earlier confiscation order (whether under PoCA 2002 or earlier legislation).

The structure of confiscation under PoCA 2002 is that the defendant's benefit of particular criminal conduct is limited to the benefit obtained as a result of, or in connection with, the offences of which he has been convicted in the current proceedings (and any offences admitted and taken into consideration in sentencing)[399].

The defendant's benefit of general criminal conduct, in contrast, is the (actual and assumed) benefit obtained as a result of, or in connection with, all the offences he has ever committed[400].

Two things follow from this. Firstly, the defendant's benefit of general criminal conduct includes his benefit of particular criminal conduct[401]. Secondly, his benefit of general criminal conduct will include benefit which has been the subject of any earlier confiscation orders against him.

There is a widespread misunderstanding to the effect that the benefit of general criminal conduct is limited to that which arises after the 'relevant day' referred to in s10 in relation to the statutory assumptions. That is not the case. There is no basis for that in the statute and case law expressly confirms that not to be the case[402].

---

[399] s76(3) & (4)

[400] s76(2) & (4)

[401] *Jawad v R [2013] EWCA Crim 644* at para [25]

[402] *Jawad v R [2013] EWCA Crim 644* at para [26]

The provisions of s8

The provisions of s8 operate in order to avoid the same benefit being subject to confiscation a second time where a defendant faces a criminal lifestyle confiscation order based on the benefit of his general criminal conduct (and has previously been the subject of a confiscation order). But these provisions are not straightforward or well-known and are sometimes overlooked by the court[403].

Subsections (5) to (8), taken together with subsections (1) & (2), in effect require the court, when making a confiscation order based on the defendant's benefit of his general criminal conduct, to deduct the total of the amounts he has previously been ordered to pay by earlier confiscation orders from the total of his benefit of general criminal conduct.

Subsections (5)(b) & (7) are necessary because a 'confiscation order' is defined by s88(6)(a) as an order under s6, and so the term does not cover a confiscation order made under other legislation.

The outcome is that, at most, the total which the defendant is ordered to pay by all the confiscation orders against him is the total of the (actual and assumed) benefit obtained by him from all his offences.

One effect of this is that, where a defendant is now to be subject to a criminal lifestyle confiscation order and the amount of an earlier confiscation order against him has been limited by his 'available amount' – so that there has been benefit previously found by the court which the defendant has not been ordered to pay – then that 'outstanding' benefit will fall to be included in the benefit to be reflected in the new confiscation order.

An example may help to illustrate the process. Jim was subject to a confiscation order in 2010. His benefit then was £100,000 and his available amount was £20,000. Jim was ordered to pay £20,000. There have been no variations to that order. In 2018 Jim was charged with a

---

[403] *R v Cole [2018] EWCA Crim 888* is an example of a case in which the provisions of s8 were apparently overlooked

criminal lifestyle offence. He was subsequently convicted. When making the confiscation order against him in 2020 the court finds that his benefit of this offence was £50,000 and there was a further £250,000 of assumed benefit since the 'relevant day' in 2012.

Jim's total benefit under the confiscation order to be made in 2020 will therefore be £380,000 comprising £50,000 benefit of the offence, £250,000 assumed benefit since 2012, and £100,000 benefit established in 2010, minus the £20,000 he has previously been ordered to pay.

If Jim has not actually paid the amount required to be paid under the confiscation order made in 2010 then the usual steps may be taken to enforce payment of the amount outstanding under that order.

However it would not be appropriate for a s22 application to be made to require a variation of the 2010 order, because the 'outstanding' benefit is now being dealt with under the 2020 order.

When seen in this context the logic of sections 8(3) & (4) becomes clear. Where the court makes a criminal lifestyle confiscation order, the benefit identified in that order must be taken to be the entirety of the defendant's benefit from his general criminal conduct up to the day on which the order is made.

This legislation has caused difficulties for prosecutors where they have failed to recognise the entirety of a defendant's benefit from his general criminal conduct when applying for a criminal lifestyle confiscation order.

That was illustrated in the case of *Chahal and Chahal*[404] where a criminal lifestyle confiscation order had been made against the defendants in respect of one offence, but other (much more serious) offending which had not, at that time, resulted in a conviction was ignored. Following a later conviction for the more serious offending, it was not open to the prosecution to include in those later confiscation proceedings benefit which had arisen to these defendants from the more serious offending

---

[404] *R v Chahal & another [2014] EWCA Crim 101*

167

prior to the making of the earlier criminal lifestyle confiscation order against them.

As a result the bulk of the benefit from the more serious offending could not be the subject of confiscation.

Avoiding overlapping periods covered by the statutory assumptions

An additional issue can arise where both the earlier and the later confiscation orders are based on the defendant's benefit of general criminal conduct.

If the making of the second 'criminal lifestyle' order follows too closely after the making of the first confiscation order there would (in the absence of legislation to prevent it) be a risk of some of the s10 assumptions being applied twice to the same period, resulting in duplication of benefit.

This potential of overlapping periods covered by the statutory assumptions is avoided by subsection 10(9)(a) which provides that, in these circumstances, the 'relevant day' cannot be earlier than the day on which the latest previous criminal lifestyle confiscation order was made against the defendant.

In consequence of s8(2) when the previous confiscation order was made it included (or is treated as having included) benefit arising to the defendant at any time up to, and including, benefit arising on the day on which that confiscation order was made[405].

If a new criminal lifestyle confiscation order is to be made stemming from the defendant being charged within six years of the making of the previous confiscation order – so that ordinarily the 'relevant day' would fall prior to the day on which the previous confiscation order had been

---

[405] In practice this would be almost impossible to achieve because it may require the prosecution preparing updated computations of benefit on the day the court was making the order.

made – then instead, as a result of s10(9)(a), the 'relevant day' will become the day on which the previous confiscation order was made.

Since the first[406] and third[407] assumptions under s10 (regarding transfers to the defendant and expenditure by him) apply to the period after the relevant day, they will then commence to operate on the day after the previous confiscation order was made and any overlap is avoided.

The position with regard to the second assumption[408] (regarding assets held after the date of conviction) is a little more difficult to resolve satisfactorily. The legislation[409] provides that, in these circumstances, the second assumption shall not apply to property held by the defendant "on or before the relevant day". The relevant day in these circumstances will be the day on which the previous confiscation order was made.

The second assumption applies to property held by the defendant after the date of his conviction (which here refers to his latest conviction).

Again the intention seems to be to avoid the same property being caught more than once by the statutory assumption. However it would appear to be a (possibly unintended) consequence that where property has been held continuously and has increased in value since the earlier confiscation order was made, that increase in value will not be within the reach of the subsequent confiscation order for the purposes of calculating assumed benefit.

---

[406] s10(2)

[407] s10(4)

[408] s10(3)

[409] s10(9)(b)

CHAPTER TWENTY-ONE

ACCOUNT FREEZING AND FORFEITURE ORDERS

Section 16 of the Criminal Finances Act 2017 inserted Chapter 3B into the Proceeds of Crime Act 2002 and introduced what is almost certainly the most significant addition to the powers available under POCA; the Account Freezing and Forfeiture Order ("**AFO**"). The reason that the AFO regime is of such significance is that it allows for the freezing of bank accounts by a Magistrates' Court on the basis of a very low level of suspicion.

Moreover, a party applying for an AFO will not be subject to anything like the level of careful scrutiny that they would face in a Crown Court Application for a Restraint Order or a High Court application for a freezing and/or proprietary injunction. This is a surprising feature of the AFO regime, as the amounts that are being frozen by government agencies are, in some cases, well in excess of £10m.

Never before has litigation, either criminal or civil, concerning such substantial sums of money been permitted outside of the Crown Court and the High Court.

What is an AFO?

The definition of an AFO is an order that, subject to exclusion, prohibits each person by or for whom the account to which the order applies is operated from making withdrawals or payments from the account. An account is said to be operated by or for a person if the person is an account holder or a signatory or identified beneficiary in relation to the account: s.303Z1(3)(a) and s.303Z1(3)(b).

Schedule 1 to the Interpretation Act 1978 is clear that references to person, "…includes a body of persons corporate or unincorporate." Schedule 2 s.4(5) states that:

"The definition of 'person' so far as it includes bodies corporate, applies to any provision of any Act whenever passed relating to an offence punishable on indictment or on summary conviction."

It follows that the freezing of a company's account is permissible under the AFO regime.

The Application

An officer applying for an AFO must fall within the definition of an enforcement officer pursuant to s.303Z1(6). They must also be authorised by a senior officer as defined at s.202Z2(4). Pursuant to s.303Z1(1) an enforcement officer can apply for an AFO if they have reasonable grounds for suspecting that money held in an account is recoverable property or is intended by any person for use in unlawful conduct.

It is important to recognise that the initial application will be made *ex parte* and that the respondent to the order will only become aware of the AFO once they have been served with notice. The respondent is, of course, entitled to apply for variation or discharge, as explained below, but POCA does not impose the same duties of full and frank disclosure etc. that will be familiar to those that are engaged in applications for High Court freezing orders or Restraint orders before the Crown Court. That being said, it is almost certain that the higher courts will expect AFO applicants to adopt that approach to ensure procedural fairness.

The Test

Firstly, the Court must be satisfied that the credit balance of the account is at least £1,000, as that is the minimum amount specified at s.303Z8(1) to justify the imposition of an AFO.

The test to be applied by the court on an application for an AFO is whether the court is satisfied on the balance of probabilities that there are reasonable grounds for suspecting the money is recoverable property or intended by any person for use in unlawful conduct. It is important to note that as an AFO is asserted to be *in rem* as opposed to *in personam* relief, many of the usual safeguards are absent.

Releasing Frozen Funds to Pay Legal Expenses

This is permitted by s.303Z(5), which provides for an exclusion from an AFO to pay reasonable legal expenses. If such an application is to be made, the Respondent should prepare a statement of assets that demonstrates that they have no other assets available that would facilitate the payment of reasonable legal expenses. That said, there is usually little difficulty in obtaining release of an initial sum of £3,000 for the purposes of providing initial advice[410].

Recoverable Property

"Recoverable property" is defined by s.304(1) of Part 5 POCA, as property that is obtained through unlawful conduct[411] and property which represents such property[412]. Unlawful conduct is defined at s.241 as conduct that is unlawful under the criminal law in the following circumstances:

> *(1) Conduct occurring in any part of the United Kingdom is unlawful conduct if it is unlawful under the criminal law of that part*

> *(2) Conduct which—*

> > *(a) occurs in a country or territory outside the United Kingdom and is unlawful under the criminal law applying in that country or territory, and*

---

[410] See the CPR Practice Direction on Civil Recovery, which applies to AFO cases by virtue of s.303Z(5)(c) POCA

[411] See Angus v United Kingdom Border Agency [2011] EWHC 461 (Admin) and *Fletcher v Chief Constable of Leicester Constabulary* [2013] EWHC 3357 with reference to the definition of "unlawful conduct".

[412] s 305

(b) if it occurred in a part of the United Kingdom, would be unlawful under the criminal law of that part, is also unlawful conduct.

(2A) Conduct which—

(a) occurs in a country or territory outside the United Kingdom,

(b) constitutes, or is connected with, the commission of a gross human rights abuse or violation (see section 241A), and

(c) if it occurred in a part of the United Kingdom, would be an offence triable under the criminal law of that part on indictment only or either on indictment or summarily, is also unlawful conduct.

(3) The court or sheriff must decide on a balance of probabilities whether it is proved—

(a) that any matters alleged to constitute unlawful conduct have occurred, or

(b) that any person intended to use any cash or property in unlawful conduct.

Maximum Term

An AFO can be made for up to two years and will automatically come to an end once that period has expired.

Variation and Discharge

An AFO can be varied by an enforcement officer or any person affected by the order on application to the court. Variations can include the provision of reasonable living expenses, the carrying on of any trade or a release to meet legal expenses (s.303Z5).

Forfeiture Order

During the currency of an AFO the applicant can apply for an Account Forfeiture Order. This can be achieved in the following two ways:

(i) the applicant serves notice on an interested party, but this is only appropriate where it is believed that there will be no objection to the application; or

(ii) the applicant applies for forfeiture and seek directions for a full forfeiture hearing.

Notice of Forfeiture

The notice of forfeiture must be served on the respondent in compliance with the Home Office Regulation. The respondent will then have 30 days from the day after service of the notice to object. That period can be extended where a party is able to explain the reason for the period elapsing; s.303Z12. It is then for the respondent to the forfeiture application to satisfy the court that the order should not have been made in respect of all or part of the money. If the respondent fails to object, the applicant can apply for the money to be forfeited (s.303Z14).

Appeal

An appeal against the making of an Account Freezing or Forfeiture order is to be made to the Crown Court. There is a 30-day time limit for appeal. In the event that the appeal is successful the owner of the account can apply for compensation from the investigatory body.

APPENDIX ONE

SECTION 18 RESPONSE

PROVISION OF FINANCIAL INFORMATION

(Section 18 Proceeds of Crime Act 2002)

R v John Doe

I, John Doe (1/1/2000) currently of HMP Widebridge, hereby provide disclosure of my financial circumstances in response to the Section 18 Order served upon me.

I expressly rely upon the protection against self-incrimination afforded by Section 18(9).

i.   Defendant's full name, date of birth, national insurance number and current address.

John Doe, 1 January 2020, AB 123456 C, currently incarcerated at HMP Widebridge, previously at 25 New Road, Widebridge WE3 2AH.

ii. Details of income, whether declared or undeclared for tax purpose including details of any employment and income for the period of six years preceding the date when these proceedings commenced.

Until my arrest I was employed by Builders of Widebridge Ltd and before that by Widebridge Plumbers Ltd. As I am currently in prison I do not have details of my income or my payslips.

I have also received student loans.

iii. Details of all property and land, freehold or leasehold, owned both in the United Kingdom and abroad, whether held in the defendant's sole name, jointly or with others or nominees or in which the defendant has an interest, (or in relation to which the defendant has used any alias name) and extent of that interest.

I do not own any property or land.

iv. Details of all motor vehicles owned or possessed whether held in the defendant's sole name, jointly with others or in which the defendant has an interest, (or in relation to which the defendant has used any alias name).

I do not currently own any vehicles.

My employer allowed me to use a van which I did not own.

v. Details of bank accounts, or deposits with licensed deposit takers in the United Kingdom or abroad, whether held in the defendant's sole name, jointly with other or in relation to which the defendant is an authorised signatory, (or in relation to which the defendant has used any alias name) including any crypto-currency accounts.

I have a Barminster Bank account. I do not know the account number. I do not have bank statements in prison. I believe there is a small balance in the account.

I also have an account with Cestershire Bank in Widebridge. Again I do not know the account number. I believe there is about £2,000.00 in this account.

vi. Details of all Credit or Debit card accounts, whether held in the defendant's sole name, jointly with others or in relation to which the defendant is an authorised signatory, (or in relation to which the defendant has used any alias name).

I owe about £500 on a credit card with Barminster Bank.

I do not know the card number.

vii. Details of all UK shares and Equities, securities, bonds, unit trusts or any foreign equivalents held by the defendant whether held in the defendant's sole name, jointly with others or in any nominee names, (or in relation to which the defendant has used any alias name).

None

viii. Details of all insurance policies where there is a financial benefit at the end of the term whether held on the defendant's life, joint on another life, or any other person's life, (or in relation to which the defendant has used any alias name).

None

ix. Details of any deposits of cash, whether in safety deposit boxes or in any other place.

The police took the cash I had on me when arrested.

x. Details of all safety deposit boxes held whether in the United Kingdom or abroad, whether held in the defendant's sole name, jointly with others or in relation to which the defendant has authorised access, (or in relation to which the defendant has used any alias name.)

None

xi. Details of any other realisable assets held by the defendant, whether held in the defendant's sole name, jointly with others or in which the defendant has an interest, (or in relation to which the defendant has used any alias name).

Nothing except my clothes and household furniture

xii. Details of any Limited company assets in relation to which the defendant is a director, the majority shareholder, or has a controlling interest in that company.

None

xiii. Details of any financial commitments and debts of the defendant.

None

xiv. Details of all transfers by way of gift or for any consideration, which is inadequate, made by the defendant, his servants or agents for the period of six years, preceding the date when theses proceedings were commenced by a third party. Such details to include the date of such transfer, the value thereof and sufficient particulars of the recipient of such transfers, to enable the same to be identified.

None

Signed: ……………………………

Name: ……………………………

Date: ……………………………..

APPENDIX TWO

SECTION 16(3) STATEMENT

IN THE CROWN COURT **INDICTMENT**

AT WIDEBRIDGE **TRIAL NO. T20210001**

STATEMENT OF INFORMATION RELEVANT IN ACCORDANCE WITH SECTION 16 (3) OF THE PROCEEDS OF CRIME ACT 2002

REGINA

V

John DOE

STATEMENT DETAILS

Prepared By : **Peter JONES**

Address : **Economic Crime Unit**
FHQ, Widebridge
WE1 2AA

Signature

Date : **1 November 2021**

Statement Tendered By

Prosecutor :

Address : **The Crown Prosecution Service**
Proceeds of Crime Unit
Pre-Enforcement North
5th Floor Zone A
102 Petty France
London
SW1H 9EA

1 Statement of Information

1.1 The prosecutor has requested that the Court proceed to confiscation under Section 6 (3(a)), or the Court has considered it appropriate so to do under Section 6 (3(b)), of the Proceeds of Crime Act 2002 (hereinafter called the Act).

1.2 It is considered appropriate for the court to proceed under Section 6(4), as it is believed that the defendant has a criminal lifestyle as defined, and that it is therefore appropriate for the Court to make the assumptions under Section 10 of the Act in determining the defendant's benefit. The defendant is believed to have a criminal lifestyle as:

- The defendant has been convicted of a schedule 2 offence as defined in POCA 2002 (S75 (2(a)).

1.3 The Court is therefore required to decide if the defendant has a criminal lifestyle. If the court decides the defendant has a criminal lifestyle it is required to decide if he has benefited from his general criminal conduct. If the court decides the defendant does not have a criminal lifestyle the court must decide if he has benefited from his particular criminal conduct

1.4   This is the statement of information dealing with all matters relevant by Peter JONES an accredited Financial Investigator into the financial affairs of John DOE (hereinafter referred to as the defendant) for the purposes of establishing

      a)   The benefit derived by the defendant

      b)   The nature of the defendant's available property, so far as it is known to me, from which any Confiscation Order made by the Court may be satisfied.

2   Civil Proceedings

2.1   Section 6(6) of the Act indicates that the duty of the court outlined in Section 6(5) becomes a power if it believes that any victim of the conduct has at any time started or intends to start proceedings against the defendant in respect of any loss, injury or damage sustained in connection with the conduct.

2.2   I am not aware of any civil proceedings against the defendant in this case.

3   Summary of Offence

3.1   On the 31st March 2021 the defendant pleaded guilty at Widebridge Crown Court to the count on the indictment of Possession with intent to supply a controlled drug of class B cannabis.

3.2   The circumstances of the offence are that on …..

3.3   On 7 November 2020 DOE was charged with the offence of Possession of a controlled drug with intent to supply. The relevant day is therefore 8 November 2014.

4   Valuation of Drugs

4.1   The recovered drugs have been examined and found to contain the following:

4.2   Exhibit ABC/03 contained 1,443.22 grams of Cannabis. This quantity of drug has been valued by DC GREEN on the basis of 1,443 (1g) street deals at £10 per deal. A total of £14,430.00. A witness statement of DC GREEN, an expert in the valuation of drugs, is attached as Appendix A.

5   Personal History

5.1   John DOE (1/1/2000) is a 21-year-old single man. I do not have any other details of his personal circumstances.

5.2   DOE has not previously been subject to confiscation.

6   Legitimate Sources of Income

6.1   The defendant has declared the following income to HM Revenue & Customs.

Tax Year	Employer	Gross Income	Student Loan
2015/16	No employment details		
2016/17	Widebridge Plumbers Ltd	6,234.00	
2017/18	Widebridge Plumbers Ltd	7,548.19	
2018/19	Widebridge Plumbers Ltd	8,121.45	7,000.00
2019/20	Widebridge Plumbers Ltd Builders of Widebridge Ltd	113.08 4,420.18	6,000.00
2020/21			4,000.00

7   Financial Record Examination

7.1   The defendant is the holder of a Barminster Bank account number (12-34-56) 87654321. This account is funded by cash credits, third party credits and inter account transfers. The account has a current credit balance of £75.30.

7.2   The defendant is the holder of a Cestershire Bank account number (65-43-21) 12345678. This account is funded by third party credits and inter account transfers. The account has a current credit balance of £2,473.00.

8   Restraint Order

8.1   No Restraint Order has been obtained in this case.

9   Extent of Benefit from Criminal Conduct

9.1   Benefit derived from Charges

9.2   The total amount of benefit obtained by this defendant as a result of the offence in these proceedings is calculated as follows:

Benefit derived as a result of the offences as charged – PWITS Cannabis £14,430.00

9.3   In accordance with S80(2)(a) of the act the benefit figure will be adjusted to take account of the increase in the value of money since the date of seizure (a copy of the calculation is attached as Appendix B).

Adjustment under S80(2)(a) of the act   £304.20

Total benefit   £14,734.20

9.4   Assumptions

A   **Property transferred to the defendant after the relevant day**

i.   The defendant is the holder of a Barminster Bank account number 87654321. This account received a series of cash credits between 2017 to 2020 which total £11,265.00 (a copy of those transactions is attached as Appendix C). The source of the cash credits is unidentified and as such it is assumed that they represent a benefit to the defendant from his general criminal conduct.

ii.   The figure of £11,265.00 has been adjusted in accordance with S80(2)(a) of the Act to take account of the increase in the value of money (a copy of the calculation is attached as Appendix D). The figure is now £11,438.37.

iii.   The defendant is the holder of a Cestershire Bank account number 12345678. This account received a series of third-party credits to the account. The third-party credits since the relevant day total £61,574.54 (a copy of those transactions is attached as Appendix E). The source of the third-party credits is unidentified and as such it is assumed that they represent a benefit to the defendant from his general criminal conduct.

iv.   The figure of £61,574.54 has been adjusted in accordance with S80(2)(a) of the Act to take account of the increase in the value of money (a copy of the calculation is attached as Appendix F). The figure is now £64,016.93.

As the source of the above transfers has not been identified, then in accordance with Section 10(2) of the Proceeds of Crime Act 2002 the Court shall assume that the money has come from the defendant's criminal conduct unless:

the assumption is shown to be incorrect

or

there would be a serious risk of injustice
if the assumption were made

B   Property held at any time after the date of conviction

i.   Recovered at the time of the defendant's arrest was the sum of
£80.00 the source of this cash is unknown. The cash was seized
and is detained. It is assumed that this money represents a
benefit from the general defendant's criminal conduct.

As the source of the above property has not been identified, then in
accordance with Section 10(3) of the Proceeds of Crime Act 2002 the
Court shall assume that the money has come from the defendant's
criminal conduct unless

the assumption is shown to be incorrect

or

there would be a serious risk of injustice
if the assumption were made

C   Expenditure incurred after the relevant day

i.   No Assumptions made under this section.

D   Valuation (Free Property)

i.   This assumption is utilized to allow property subject to the
assumptions to be valued.

ii.   For the purposes of valuing any property obtained (or assumed to have been obtained) by the defendant, he obtained it free of any other interests in it.

In accordance with Section 16(4(b)) of the Proceeds of Crime Act 2002 I confirm that I am not aware of any information that would cause the court not to make the statutory assumptions.

10   Summary of Benefit

10.1 Table of Benefit

Source	Detail	Amount
Benefit from conviction	Offence charged	14,734.20
Assumptions		
Transfers	Cash Credits to Barminster account	11,438.37
	Third-party credits to Cestershire account	64,016.93
Property held	Recovered Cash	80.00
Expenditure	No assumptions made	0.00
	Total Benefit	**90,269.50**

11   Known Available Amount

11.1   The onus is on the defendant to provide the Court with full details of all his free property, including full internal valuations (carried out by a professional valuer) for any houses he has an interest in. He will also need to supply the Court with details of the likely costs that will be incurred in realising the property.

11.2 The free property that I have identified is as follows:

11.3 The cash recovered at the time of the defendant's arrest which amounted to £80.00.

11.4 Recovered at the time of the defendant's arrest were a quantity of items of designer clothing (details of the items are contained in the schedule at Appendix G). I have valued the clothing on a second hand basis at £1,590.00.

11.5 The defendant is the holder of a Barminster Bank account number 87654321. The account has a current credit balance of £75.30.

11.6 The defendant is the holder of a Cestershire Bank account number 12345678. The account has a current credit balance of £2,473.00.

11.7 The above assets and their valuations are provided for the assistance of the Court. The onus remains with the defendant to show, with evidence that he does not have sufficient assets to meet the benefit.

11.8 Summary of Assets

Asset	Details of any third party interest	Amount
Recovered cash	No third-party interest known.	80.00
Designer Clothing	No third-party interest known.	1,590.00
Barminster Bank account number 87654321	No third-party interest known.	75.30
Cestershire Bank account number 12345678	No third-party interest known.	2,473.00
		4,218.30

12   Proportionality

12.1   The Court is required not to make a confiscation order insofar as such an order would be disproportionate and thus a breach of Article 1, Protocol 1.

12.2   I am not aware of any issues which should be brought to the Court's attention and which would affect the proportionality of the order.

13   Defence Response

13.1   Section 17 of the Act allows the Court to order that the defendant respond to the Prosecution statement indicating the extent to which he accepts each allegation and to give particulars of any matters upon which he relies. If the defendant fails to comply with such an order he may be treated as accepting every allegation apart from any allegation he has replied to or any allegation that he has benefited from his general or particular criminal conduct.

13.2   Any reply to this statement made under the Proceeds of Crime Act 2002 should be served on Widebridge Crown Court, and a copy sent to the Crown Prosecution Service.

13.3   On .... the court ordered the defence to serve a reply to this statement by .....

14   Confiscation Order

14.1   If the Court accepts that the defendant has benefited from the proceeds of crime to the extent of £90,269.50 then the court should declare the benefit in that amount, or in any other amount in respect of which the court finds the defendant has benefited.

14.2   The recoverable amount is an amount equal to the Defendant's benefit from the conduct concerned. If the defendant shows that the available amount is less than the benefit, the court should make a confiscation order in that sum. (Section 7 POCA 2002)

15 Effect of Confiscation on Court's Other Powers

15.1 Section 13 of POCA states that the Court must take account of the confiscation order before it imposes a fine or makes an order involving payment by the defendant other than a priority order as set out at Section 13(3). The effect of Section 13 (5) of the Act permits the Court to make a priority order as if a confiscation order had not been made.

15.2 If the defendant cannot pay both orders, the priority order must be recovered from sums paid in satisfaction of the confiscation order. (Section 13(6) POCA 2002).

16 Time to Pay

16.1 Section 11 of the Act states that a confiscation order must be paid on the day on which the order is made. However where the defendant shows that he requires time to pay, the Court may order payment within a specified period, or within specified periods each of which relates to a specified amount. A specified period must start with the date the confiscation order is made and must not exceed three months from the date the order is made.

17 Compliance Orders

17.1 Section 13A(2) of the Act states that a court may make such orders as it believes is appropriate for the purpose of ensuring that the confiscation order is effective (a "compliance order").

APPENDIX THREE

SECTION 17 RESPONSE

In The Widebridge Crown Court

T2021/0001

Made on Behalf of the Defendant

BETWEEN:

REGINA

-v-

JOHN DOE

===

SECTION 17 STATEMENT OF JOHN DOE IN RESPONSE TO CONFISCATION PROCEEDINGS BROUGHT BY THE CROWN

===

I, JOHN DOE, currently of HMP Widebridge, Widebridge, WE10 7XZ will say as follows:

1.   I am the Defendant in Confiscation Proceedings brought against me at the behest of the Crown, pursuant to Section 6 of the Proceeds of Crime Act 2002 ("POCA"). This statement has been prepared in response to the Statement of Information ("SOI") that has been served by the Crown, purportedly in compliance with Section 16(3) of POCA.

2.   Unless otherwise identified, I have direct knowledge of the facts set out in this statement and I believe those facts to be true. Where information has been provided by third parties, I identify the source of that information and believe the information provided to me to be true. Where in this statement I refer to legal advice, or to communications with third parties for the dominant purpose of these proceedings, this should not be regarded as a waiver of privilege

3.   The abbreviations, and headings set out in the SOI are generally adopted in this statement in response, and for convenience it is organised in the same way as the SOI but no admissions are made thereby.

4.   Having pleaded guilty on 31 March 2021, I was convicted of one Count of Possessing a controlled drug of Class B with intent to supply, contrary to Section 5(3) of the Misuse of Drugs Act 1971.

5.   These Confiscation Proceedings follow that conviction.

6.   I strongly contest the allegation that all of the identified property and bank accounts referred to within the SOI, represents benefit derived from the proceeds of crime.

1.   **Statement of Information**

7.   Paragraphs 1.1 to 1.3 are admitted, save that it is disputed that it is appropriate for the Court to make the relevant assumptions under s.10 POCA in relation to the totality of the assets identified by the Crown and it is denied that the Defendant has a criminal lifestyle.

8.   Paragraph 1.4 is admitted, save that no admission is made as to whether the SOI deals with all relevant matters. That is a matter for the Financial Investigator and outside of the knowledge of the Defendant. No admission is made as to the adequacy of the SOI.

2.   **Civil Proceedings**

9.   Paragraph 2.1 is admitted.

10.   As to paragraph 2.2, the Defendant is equally unaware of any independent civil proceedings having been brought by any party.

3.   **Summary of Offence**

11.   Paragraph 3.1 is admitted.

12.   As to paragraph 3.2, the circumstances of the offence are admitted, save that:

    (1)   It is denied that [....]

    (2)   It is denied that [...]

    (3)   It is denied that [...]

13.   Paragraph 3.3 is admitted.

4.   **Valuation of drugs**

14.   As to paragraph 4.1:

(1)   The fact of the examination of the drugs is admitted.

(2)   The finding that the total weight of the cannabis seized was [...] is denied. .

(3)   It is denied that ...

15.   Paragraph 4.2. is denied. The defendant does not accept the valuation of the drugs seized and will instruct an independent drug valuation expert to provide a valuation. In particular the defendant does not accept that these drugs were to be sold in 1 gram street deals.

5.   **Personal History**

16.   Paragraphs 5.1 and 5.2 are admitted. He has one child, Deirdre Doe (born 28/2/2019), with his domestic partner, Julie Black

6.   **Legitimate Sources of Income**

17.   Paragraph 6.1 is admitted.

7.   **Financial Record Examination**

18.   Paragraphs 7.1 and 7.2 are admitted, save that reference should be made to the Defendant's further comments in respect of assumed benefit.

8.   **Restraint Order**

19.   Paragraph 8.1 is admitted.

9.   **Extent of Benefit from Criminal Conduct**

20.   As to paragraph 9.1 to 9.3:

    (1)   The valuation of the drugs is not accepted. See paragraph 15 above.

    (2)   The CPIH uplift is not accepted, pending examination by a forensic accountant.

    (3)   The assumed benefit of property transferred to the defendant after the relevant day is not accepted. A forensic accountant is being instructed and the detailed figures will be addressed when his report has been received.

    (4)   The cash of £80.00 seized at the time of the defendant's arrest belongs to his domestic partner and therefore is not property held by the defendant and is not benefit of his.

21.   As to paragraph 9.4:

10. <u>Summary of Benefit</u>

22. The benefit figure of £90,269.50 is denied for the reasons set out above.

11. <u>Known Available Amount</u>

23. As to paragraph 11:

(1) Subject to practical considerations, no issue is taken with paragraph 11.1.

(2) No admission is made to paragraph 11.2.

(3) As to paragraph 11.3:

(i) It is admitted that £80 of cash was seized at the time of the defendant's arrest;

(ii) It is denied that this cash is recoverable property. It belongs to his domestic partner and, therefore, is not property held by the defendant and is not a component of his available amount.

(4) As to paragraph 11.4:

(i) It is admitted that the Defendant possessed clothing, but no admission is made as to whether those items can be properly categorised or described as, "designer clothing"

(ii) It is denied that the second-hand value of that clothing amounts £1,590.00.

(5) As to paragraph 11.5, the Defendant accepts that he has an account at Barminster Bank, but this is not restrained and monies are required from it to support his domestic partner and their young daughter. The figure will inevitably require adjustment before the confiscation hearing.

(6) As to paragraph 11.6, the Defendant accepts that he has an account at Cestershire Bank, but this is not restrained and monies are required from it to support his domestic partner

and their young daughter. The figure will inevitably require adjustment before the confiscation hearing.

(7)   Paragraph 11.7 is admitted, save that it is for the Crown to prove the accuracy of the benefit figure that it contends for in these proceedings.

(8)   Paragraph 11.8 is denied for the reasons set out above.

12.   **Proportionality**

24.   Paragraph 12 is admitted.

13.   **Defence Response**

25.   No issue is taken with paragraphs 13.1 to 13.3, save that it should be noted that the Court granted an extension for the section 17 response to be served by [day] [month] 2022. The defence reserve the right to add to or amend this statement on receipt of further material.

14.   **Confiscation Order**

26.   Paragraph 14.1 is denied. The Defendant does not accept the benefit figure in the Section 16(3) statement for the reasons noted above.

27.   Paragraph 14.2 is denied. The defendant does not accept the available amount figure in the Section 16(3) statement for the reasons noted above.

15.   **Effect of Confiscation on Court's Other Powers**

28.   Paragraph 15 is noted.

16.   **Time to Pay**

29.   Paragraph 16 is noted.

17.   **Compliance Orders**

30.   Paragraph 17 is noted.

STATEMENT OF TRUTH

I believe that the facts stated in this Witness Statement are true.

SIGNED:

      John Doe

Dated: […]

APPENDIX FOUR

SCOTT SCHEDULE

IN THE WIDEBRIDGE CROWN COURT

INDICTMENT NO: T2021/0001

IN THE PROCEEDS OF CRIME ACT 2002

BETWEEN:

REGINA   Claimant

v

JOHN DOE   Defendant

SCOTT SCHEDULE –

SECTION 6 PROCEEDS OF CRIME ACT 2002

BENEFIT

Description	Per prosecution	Per defence	Court
Drugs seized	1,443g cannabis @ £10 per gram (street deal value) £14,430.00	1,443g cannabis @ £4 per gram (wholesale value per expert) £5,772.00	
CPIH uplift	£304.20	£121.68	
Barminster Bank credits – account 87654321	Cash credits £11,265.00	Cash credits – excluding rebankings & legitimate cash £4505.00	
CPIH uplift	£173.37	£70.22	
Cestershire Bank credits – account 12345678	Third party credits £61,575.54	Third party credits – excluding partner's income & legitimate credits £42,269.33	
CPIH uplift	£2,442.39	£1,702.03	
Cash seized on arrest	Found in defendant's home £80.00	Cash belongs to partner £0.00	
TOTAL BENEFIT	£90,269.50	£54,440.26	

AVAILABLE AMOUNT

Description	Per prosecution	Per defence	Court
Cash seized on arrest	Found in defendant's home £80.00	Cash belongs to partner £0.00	
Designer clothing	Estimated second-hand value £1,590.00	Estimated to realise £50.00	
Barminster Bank balance – account 87654321	Balance at 3 September 2021 £75.30	Balance at 21 January 2022 (per bank statement) £5.30	
Cestershire Bank balance – account 12345678	Balance at 14 September 2021 £2,473.00	Balance at 19 January 2022 (per bank statement) £1,320.67	
TOTAL AVAILABLE AMOUNT	**£4,218.30**	**£1,375.97**	

APPENDIX FIVE

SECTION 23 APPLICATION

J Doe
Applicant
JD 1
4 November 20…

<u>IN THE WIDEBRIDGE CROWN COURT</u>

T20210001

B E T W E E N:

JOHN DOE

<u>Applicant</u>

- and -

REGINA

<u>Respondent</u>

WITNESS STATEMENT OF JOHN DOE IN SUPPORT OF AN APPLICATION PURSUANT TO SECTION 23 OF THE PROCEEDS OF CRIME ACT 2002

I, John Doe, will say as follows:

1. I make this witness statement in compliance with Criminal Procedure Rule 33.17 and pursuant to s.23 of the Proceeds of Crime Act 2002 ("POCA"). I am the subject of a confiscation order made by HHJ […] on [date]. That confiscation order records the learned judge's finding that the calculated benefit figure is £78,174.60 and the available amount is £2,405.97. At present, I must pay the sum of £2,405.97 in satisfaction of the confiscation order or face a sentence of 2 months' imprisonment in default.

2. Unless otherwise identified, I have direct knowledge of the facts set out in this witness statement and I believe those facts to be true. Where information has been provided to me by my third parties, I identify the source of that information and believe the information provided to me to be true. Where in this witness statement I refer to legal advice, or to communications with third parties for the dominant purpose of these proceedings, this should not be regarded as a waiver of privilege. There is now shown to me and produced under the exhibits marked "JD1" a bundle of documents to which I refer below. References to page numbers are to pages of JD1.

3. This witness statement is made in support of an application for variation of my confiscation order due to the inadequacy of the available amount. In order to explain the timing of this application, I set out below the history of the litigation that has followed the making of the confiscation order.

THE CONFISCATION ORDER

4. On […], I was sentenced to a period of […] months' imprisonment by the Widebridge Crown Court for possession with intent to supply cannabis. In passing sentence, HHJ […] determined that I had played a "significant role" in the supply of cannabis. The cannabis recovered by the police was valued at £[…]. As the Court will be aware, possession of a controlled drug of Class B with intent to supply is a Schedule 2 offence for the purposes of the Proceeds of Crime Act. The confiscation proceedings followed my conviction.

5. At the confiscation hearing HHJ […] was in possession of:

5.1 a number of statements served on my behalf in compliance with s.17 and s.18 POCA [JD/1 to JD/2]; and

5.2 the report of a forensic accountant, Mr David Winch [JD/3].

6. As the statutory assumptions applied, the burden was upon me to discharge those assumptions. I enclose a copy of HHJ [...]'s judgment at [JD/4]. It follows that I am currently liable to pay £2,405.97, as a consequence of the proceeds of crime enquiry that followed my conviction for involvement in the possession of cannabis with intent to supply.

Enforcement

7. Enforcement proceedings were commenced at the Widebridge Magistrates' Court on [date]. In short, those proceedings were adjourned on a number of occasions while efforts were made to sell the designer clothing that represents £1,000.00 of the total available amount. A further enforcement hearing is now scheduled to take place on [date].

8. Although the designer clothing has now been sold, it has only realised a value of £400.00, which means that a significant part of the confiscation order will remain outstanding.

Application for Recalculation of the Available Amount

9. It has been explained to me that an application pursuant to s.23 POCA must be directed at the reasons as to why the available amount or specific assets included within the available amount are no longer recoverable.

10. I exhibit at [JD/5] the receipts that demonstrate the actual sale value that has been realised in respect of each of the individual items of designer clothing

11. For the avoidance of doubt, I make it clear that I do not have access to any other assets that are capable of satisfying the difference between the estimated value of the designer clothing at the confiscation hearing and the value actually realised upon sale. I cannot satisfy the confiscation order in its current form and I anticipate that I will not be in a position to do so.

12. The amount originally ordered to be paid of £2,405.97 and the amounts realised may be summarised as follows:

Description	Per confiscation order (form 5050A)	Amount realised
Cash seized on arrest	£80.00	£80.00
Designer clothing	£1,000.00	£400.00
Barminster Bank balance – account 87654321	£5.30	£5.30
Cestershire Bank balance – account 12345678	£1,320.67	£1,320.67
TOTAL	£2,405.97	£1,805.97

13. For the reasons set out above, I apply pursuant to s.23 of the Proceeds of Crime Act 2002, for a recalculation of the available amount and ask that the amount required to be paid be reduced by £600.00 to a total figure of £1,805.97.

Statement of Truth

I believe that the facts stated in this witness statement are true.

SIGNED: ....

John Doe

Date: ....

MORE BOOKS BY
LAW BRIEF PUBLISHING

A selection of our other titles available now:-

'A Practical Guide to Transgender Law' by Robin Moira White & Nicola Newbegin
'Artificial Intelligence – The Practical Legal Issues (2nd Edition)' by John Buyers
'A Practical Guide to Challenging Sham Marriage Allegations in Immigration Law' by Priya Solanki
'A Practical Guide to New Build Conveyancing' by Paul Sams & Rebecca East
'A Practical Guide to Inherited Wealth on Divorce' by Hayley Trim
'A Practical Guide to Shareholder Disputes in Family Businesses' by Ed Weeks
'A Practical Guide to the Law of Forests in Scotland' by Philip Buchan
'A Practical Guide to Health and Medical Cases in Immigration Law' by Rebecca Chapman & Miranda Butler
'A Practical Guide to Bad Character Evidence for Criminal Practitioners by Aparna Rao
'A Practical Guide to Environmental Enforcement' by Christopher Badger & Stuart Jessop
'A Practical Guide to Hoarding and Mental Health for Housing Lawyers' by Rachel Coyle
'A Practical Guide to Psychiatric Claims in Personal Injury – 2nd Edition' by Liam Ryan
'Stephens on Contractual Indemnities' by Richard Stephens
'A Practical Guide to the EU Succession Regulation' by Richard Frimston
'A Practical Guide to Solicitor and Client Costs – 2nd Edition' by Robin Dunne
'Constructive Dismissal – Practice Pointers and Principles' by Benjimin Burgher
'A Practical Guide to Religion and Belief Discrimination Claims in the Workplace' by Kashif Ali
'A Practical Guide to the Law of Medical Treatment Decisions' by Ben Troke

These books and more are available to order online direct from the publisher at www.lawbriefpublishing.com, where you can also read free sample chapters. For any queries, contact us on 0844 587 2383 or mail@lawbriefpublishing.com.

Our books are also usually in stock at www.amazon.co.uk with free next day delivery for Prime members, and at good legal bookshops such as Wildy & Sons.

We are regularly launching new books in our series of practical day-to-day practitioners' guides. Visit our website and join our free newsletter to be kept informed and to receive special offers, free chapters, etc.

You can also follow us on Twitter at www.twitter.com/lawbriefpub.

Lightning Source UK Ltd.
Milton Keynes UK
UKHW021824040322
399590UK00005B/343

9 781913 715441